"Coming up to race at WIR with the best short-track racers in the country was an extremely valuable asset to my career. It is a source of great pride for me to have won two Red, White and Blue Series championships."

***- Mark Martin, one of "NASCAR's 50 Greatest Drivers"*

Wisconsin International Raceway

Where the Big Ones Run!

Joe Verdegan

M&B Global Solutions, Inc.
Green Bay, Wisconsin (USA)

Wisconsin International Raceway
Where the Big Ones Run!

© 2016 Joseph J. Verdegan

Second Edition
All Rights Reserved. The author grants no assignable permission to reproduce for resale or redistribution. This license is limited to the individual purchaser and does not extend to others. Permission to reproduce these materials for any other purpose must be obtained in writing from the publisher except for the use of brief quotations within book chapters.

Disclaimer
The views expressed in this work are solely those of the author and do not necessarily reflect the views of the publisher, and the publisher hereby disclaims any responsibility for them. In the event you use any of the information in this book for yourself, which is your constitutional right, the author and the publisher assume no responsibility for your actions.

Front cover photo:
Mark Martin leads Butch Miller, Joe Shear, Terry Baldry and Scott Hansen in a mid-1980s ARTGO race at WIR. *(ARTGO promotions photo from the Roger Van Daalwyk collection)*

Back cover photo:
Author Joe Verdegan *(Ron Nikolai photo)*

ISBN 10: 1-942731-24-8
ISBN 13: 978-1-942731-24-5

Published by M&B Global Solutions Inc.
Green Bay, Wisconsin (USA)

Dedication

This book is dedicated to the late Gary Vercauteren, public relations guru for WIR and the Fox River Racing Club for many seasons.

Gary helped put this track on the map, not only on a regional level, but also to nationwide prominence. Personally, Gary opened up many doors for me in motorsports media, both locally and regionally. Gary's passion for the sport was second to none. He was a great friend and mentor. This author learned a lot from him.

Contents

Introduction 1
Roger Van Daalwyk - *All in the Family* 5
Clyde Schumacher - *Always Smilin'* 13
Ron Leek - *Getting it Started* 19
Gary Vercauteren - *For Immediate Release* 25
Red, White and Blue State Championship Series 29
Victor Getzloff and Dick Trickle - *Life of the Party* 35
Mark Martin - *Fast out of the Box* 41
Bob Abitz - *The Flyin' School Teacher* 43
Rene Grode - *Beating the Bushes* 49
Figure 8 - *Meet in the Middle* 57
The Gracyalny Family - *Born to Race* 65
Gene Wheeler - *Cubic Dollars* 71
Rod Wheeler - *The Villain* 75
Roger Regeth - *The Bear* 81
Dixieland - *Traditional Tuesday Biggie* 85
Echoes of a Fatal Crash - *How, and Why Racing Lost Larry Detjens* 89
Alan Kulwicki/Mike Randerson - *Potent Duo* 99
Al Golueke - *Shop Rat* 109

The Long Haulers - *Windshield Time* 115
Scott Hansen - *Titletown's Racing Champion* 125
Steve Smits - *Quarter-Mile Dominance* 131
Pete Berken - *Pushing the Envelope* 135
Jim Duchow - *Racing Cop* 139
Lowell Bennett - *Family Tradition* 145
Gordie Sannes - *Loyalty* 151
Terry Baldry - *Smooth as Silk* 157
Matt Kenseth/Patty & Mike Butz - *A Star is Born* 161
Tom Goff - *Making Deadline* 167
Jim Pagel - *Gone Way Too Soon* 171
Detroit Iron - *True Parity* 179
Nuts and Bolts - WIR's Bits and Pieces 189
Mini Champs and Trucks - *Gentlemen, Pull Your Recoils* 197
Eve of Destruction - *Better Get an Early Seat* 203
WIR Honor Roll 205
Acknowledgements 211
About the Author 213

An aerial view of the newly constructed KK Sports Arena, later known as Wisconsin International Raceway, in about 1968. (Roger Van Daalwyk collection)

Introduction

I was just nine years old the first time my folks took me to Wisconsin International Raceway (WIR) in Kaukauna.

The year was 1977 and we were there for the "White Race" – the second of the three-leg Red, White and Blue State Championship Series. It was a sunny, breezy Sunday afternoon. My brother, Jesse, and I sat on a blanket on "The Hill" in turn one, while Mom and Dad sat in lawn chairs behind us.

The facility started out as KK Sports Arena before switching over to Wisconsin International Raceway in 1975. In certain chapters of this book, you'll notice I will refer to the track by either name depending on the time frame involved.

The track that day in 1977 was almost magical for me. All the big names I'd only read about as a kid in *Midwest Racing News* and *Checkered Flag Racing News* were there – live and in person. Dick Trickle from Wisconsin Rapids was there with his sparkling, SuperAmerica-sponsored number 99. So was Larry Detjens from Wausau, with his super cool, burnt orange number 25

Mopar. And Joe Shear from Clinton, who towed up with his familiar number 36 ride. And Rudolph's Tom Reffner was always there with his sleek, blue number 88 AMC Javelin.

These were the stars from Central Wisconsin that, up until my visit to WIR in 1977, I'd only seen pictures of their cars in color. Now it came to life, in full color. These guys were larger-than-life heroes in another part of the state, and I was soaking in every bit of it.

Track announcer Jim Jaeger would spell out the drivers last names phonetically over the public address system's tinny-sounding speakers during qualifying: "Car number 18, from Wisconsin Rapids driving a '77 Olds Cutlass, Mike Miller - M-I-L-L-E-R." Many race fans would write down the drivers' qualifying laps in a notebook or on a clipboard, all while soaking in the sun. Fields of forty to fifty of the state's best late model drivers converged on WIR three Sunday afternoons each race season. And back then, the Red, White and Blue races at WIR were truly "specials."

I recall as a kid sharing watermelon with Trickle in the pit area after one of the Red, White and Blue events while collecting driver autographs. The adults consumed either an ice cold Pabst Blue Ribbon or a Coors Light with Trickle (depending upon who was sponsoring him at the time.) Unlike today's NASCAR drivers, who are often insulated from the race fans (unless you've bought a VIP ticket, of course), those guys were almost *always* accessible and realized how important their fans were. The drivers often worked forty to fifty hours per week and sacrificed sleep to get to the race track on weekends. They were truly blue collar and treated their fans like gold.

It was those Red, White and Blue races which drew me to love WIR. A few years later, in 1980, my grandfather Darold Aebischer, who had retired from his duties as a flagman at area dirt ovals, took Jesse and me to every single Thursday night race at WIR that year. Grandpa, who fueled airplanes for a living at Austin Straubel Airport in Green Bay, juggled his schedule with trades and vacation days to make sure we never missed a race that summer. I'll always cherish those Thursday nights with Grandpa. I've still got a notebook full of qualifying times from that entire season.

It was not uncommon that summer to have future NASCAR stars Alan Kulwicki from Greenfield, Jim Sauter from Necedah or Ted Musgrave from Grand Marsh in a typical feature field. Couple that with local talent like Terry

Baldry of Omro, JJ Smith of Appleton or "Lightning Lowell" Bennett from Neenah, and even the studs from farther south such as Tony "The Tiger" Strupp from Slinger, Al Schill from Franklin and Johnny Ziegler from Madison.

As the years marched on, I began announcing stock car races at the local dirt tracks in the greater Green Bay area. I was announcing at 141 Speedway in Francis Creek and Seymour Speedway as a teenager. I got a lucky break in 1995 when I got a call from Kaukauna's Mike Clancy, who was president of the Fox River Racing Club. The FRRC promoted the weekly Thursday night races at WIR. Clancy, upon recommendation from the late Gary Vercauteren, who for years had handled public relations for the club, hired me to serve as the track's weekly announcer. It was a position I was fortunate enough to hold for six seasons.

I'll always remain grateful to Gary and Mike for getting me involved with WIR. I've witnessed some great races, some horrendous crashes, and met some of the most colorful characters one could ever imagine. The track and the club have a long history and tradition. What I've attempted to do with this book is recapture the sights, the smells and the sounds of what the races were like at WIR over the years.

There are those who've passed away, who I never got the chance to interview for this book. I would have loved to have had conversations with Dick Trickle, Joe Shear, Alan Kulwicki, Rich Somers, Larry Detjens, Jim Sauter, Jim Pagel, "Stan The Man" Gracyalny, Joe Van Daalwyk, Bruce Mueller, Gary Vercauteren, John and Sue McKarns, Fred Pagel, Bob Seehawer, and Bob Bergeron.

Get ready … we're going green!

Joe Verdegan
Fall 2016

*Roger Van Daalwyk (left) and Steve Carlson in 1997
(Track photos by Robert Pilsudski)*

Roger Van Daalwyk
All in the Family

Before it became one of the most prominent paved track facilities in the Midwest, Wisconsin International Raceway started out as 120 acres of woodlands, grass and hills owned by a local farmer at Highway 55 and County Highway KK in Kaukauna.

Local businessman Joe Van Daalwyk owned a construction company, among other local businesses. In 1963, Van Daalwyk partnered up with fellow Fox Valley residents Connie DeLeeuw and Clyde Schumacher and began building what initially was called KK Sports Arena. It started out as a half-mile dirt track with a paved quarter-mile oval and a Figure 8 track on the inside. The trio also built a dragstrip behind the oval and a retaining pond in the infield.

As a young teen, Van Daalwyk's son, Roger, wound up doing a little bit of everything when it came to building the facility. "He'd have me drive dump truck when I was real young – well before I had a driver's license," said Roger Van Daalwyk. "I would help build bleachers, pop popcorn and stock coolers on race day. I'd do all of the weed eating before the races and clean up all the garbage after the shows. I did most of the jobs there at some point growing up."

Roger Van Daalwyk would ride his bike as a teenager from Kaukauna to Combined Locks daily in the summer months. With visions of racing top-notch, late model stock cars on the tar, KK Sports Arena was paved in March 1968.

"They built that track as sort of a mini version of Daytona International Speedway," said Van Daalwyk.

The facility's new paved half-mile track had a surrounding four-foot concrete wall, twelve-foot banks, caution lights on the corners, painted lanes, and a "double-kiss" rail on the inside. The track featured curves that were seventy feet wide and straightaways that were sixty-five feet wide. The new model stock cars would be the showcase, and speeds in the range of 110 to 120 miles per hour on the straightaway and an average 85-90 miles per hour overall were expected.

There was permanent seating for 11,000 fans in the grandstand and room for perhaps 14,000 more on surrounding hillsides for the quarter-mile and half-mile events. The bleachers along the drag strip held around 8,500, with hillsides that could accommodate 12,000 to 15,000 overall.

The first event was a USAC race on June 2, 1968. "The place was a sellout," Van Daalwyk said. "There was no fencing back then. You bought your tickets down in the entrance way. You just bought your ticket and walked in. It was sort of like a drive-in movie theatre."

In 1969, when Joe Van Daalwyk bought Great Lakes Dragaway in Union Grove, Wisconsin, near the Wisconsin/Illinois border, Roger Van Daalwyk would travel down there to work for his dad on the bigger drag race weekends.

"Between 1966 and 1969, KK Sports Arena was doing good and holding its own," said Van Daalwyk. "In 1970, it was a season of a lot of rain and KK Sports Arena went under."

It was at that time Joe Van Daalwyk bought the struggling track back from DeLeeuw and it was renamed Wisconsin International Raceway the following year. Ted Schmalz was named the track's general manager. Roger's brother, Pat Van Daalwyk, along with Dave Lindemuth worked at the track under the new WIR banner.

Roger Van Daalwyk worked on the safety crew on the half mile. Halfway through the 1972 season, Schmalz was let go from his GM duties and Roger Van Daalwyk became the general manager of WIR at eighteen years old, just weeks after he graduated high school.

In 1972, the USAC stock car series had grown to become a pretty expensive date for track promoters. "Eventually, Dad had grown tired of the USAC boys and their demands," said Van Daalwyk. "That's when Dad hired Gary Vercauteren to handle public relations and marketing for the track."

And thus, the Red, White and Blue State Championship Series was formed.

"Gary was very, very good at what he did," said Van Daalwyk. "He really went to bat for the track."

Van Daalwyk ran a heavy rotation of ads on local radio stations, including WKAU 105 FM. "I wrote the copy for those radio ads," said Van Daalwyk. Among the catch lines in the ads where phrases like "Just a burnout south of Highway 55 in Kaukauna" or "Sunday, Sunday, Sunday!!" to promote the Red, White and Blue series races.

They'd purchase large ads frequently in local papers such as the *Appleton Post-Crescent*, the *Kaukauna Times* and racing trade publications *Midwest Racing News* and Che*ckered Flag Racing News*. "Those ads were real effective back in those days before social media and that stuff," said Van Daalwyk.

Joe Van Daalwyk eventually sold his construction company, which built WIR, and went north in the 1980s to build a fourteen-cottage resort in Lake Tomahawk.

"Dad came home from Lake Tomahawk before the White race in 1983 when he told me he had cancer," said Van Daalwyk. "I was shocked. It was race day. We're sitting on the back steps. For all those years growing up, I'd always have to knock on the door of his office to talk to him at night. He was always busy. But that day he insisted that he talk to me right away. He died at sixty-two years old. My plan was I was going to continue to run the track for him as the owner. But he passed away after Christmas that year."

Joe Van Daalwyk had a reputation as a tireless worker who expected and demanded nothing but the best.

"Dad would tell you what to do – and show you how to do it," said Roger Van Daalwyk. "And there was only one way to do it, and that was the right way. He told me there was no such thing as saying no. Anything can be done if you put your mind to it."

In the final years leading up to his death, Joe Van Daalwyk acted as a consultant to Roger in the day-to-day operations of the track. "We'd have meetings almost daily to cover every detail to make sure things were done right," said Van Daalwyk. "We are actually busier at this game in the winter time. You aren't necessarily as busy at the track per se, but the meetings to go over the track schedule, payout and tracking down sponsors goes on all winter long."

Van Daalwyk leased WIR from 1984 to 1988 from the family trust that had been set up.

"Dad had it in his will that I was either going to buy it or it was going to be sold. Nobody else in the family wanted to run it," said Van Daalwyk. "I couldn't have made that decision without consulting with my good friends John and Sue McKarns."

McKarns had owned the ARTGO Challenge series, which hosted special late model events all across the Midwest, including WIR.

"We were down in Florida at the RPM workshops, and I was leasing the track and subleasing it to John for those ARTGO shows," recalled Van Daalwyk. "After we were done in the workshops all day, we found a room and the three of us talked about it. By 9:30 p.m. that night, John had convinced me to buy WIR."

Over the years, the ARTGO Challenge series was a win-win deal for both ARTGO and WIR. WIR almost served as an anchor track of sorts for the series. Its annual events continued there with ARTGO. The advice John McKarns would give Van Daalwyk would come full circle many years later.

"We were at a promoters meeting over in La Crosse in 2014, and Gregg (McKarns, John's son) was there," said Van Daalwyk. "I had convinced Gregg to purchase Madison (International Speedway). Gregg was on the fence, but after I talked with him and reminded him that he had grown up with the sport, and that I had all the confidence in the world in him, he wound

New ARTGO President John McKarns (left) and Joe Van Daalwyk meet in the spring of 1979 to sign the first ARTGO special at WIR. That June 24, 1979, date drew over 7,000 fans to watch Bobby Allison compete. (John McKarns collection)

up buying the track."

Fox River Racing Club leases the track for Thursday Night Thunder races. Prior to 1974, the Wolf River Racing Association (WRRA) ran the program on the quarter mile, with only Red, White and Blue races on the half mile.

"I've always worked well with the club to provide affordable, family entertainment on Thursday nights," said Van Daalwyk. "Dave Valentyne, Rene Grode, Ray Dietzen and Bob Bennett are among some of the guys who ran the club in the past that are still around to this day."

With the ARTGO specials that were run at WIR, Van Daalwyk got to know many of those drivers well over the years. Here's his take on a few of them:

Mark Martin. "A very classy dude. I remember being down at the Wisconsin Fans for Auto Racing banquet in Milwaukee. Mark was there with his son, Matt, who was just a baby at the time. He was swimming with him in the pool. Just having fun. A very down-to-earth guy. When Gary Vercauteren drove Mark into the track for the first time, Mark looked down and said,

"Oooohhhh weeee! This track is gonna be fun!"

Alan Kulwicki. "Alan was all business. He never stopped working on that race car when he was at the track. He was a perfectionist. The car had to be perfect every time. It was not uncommon for Kulwicki to still be checking things like tire pressures and such while most other drivers had already popped open their coolers and had their race cars already loaded."

Rusty Wallace. "Super nice guy. He just loved racing. Heck, I remember Rusty Wallace would come and be a spectator here a few times to watch his brother Kenny race. I looked over in the stands and here's Rusty eating bratwursts and drinking Miller Lite as a fan in the stands. He just came unannounced. That was pretty cool."

Matt Kenseth. "You just knew he was going to go big. We always told Matt to remember where he came from when he hit it big in Cup racing. Matt would leave the pits after the races and go to the Pit Stop Bar and Grill. After the races, he'd always have our pizzas. He loved those pizzas. I thought he'd be really, really good, but I didn't know he'd get that big that fast."

Dick Trickle. "Some of the stuff with Trickle was exaggerated with the drinking and stuff, to be honest with you. But I'll say this: There was nobody better and dealing with the fans than Dick Trickle. He was the best, hands down. He'd stay late after the races until every last fan had left the track, signing autographs. He was always the last hauler out of the parking lot. Then, after the fans would leave, he'd say 'Okay, now it's time to have a couple of beers.' He'd pull his hauler up behind the stands. We'd go sit up in the press box, where I still had some cold beer up there. We'd go up there and solve all the world's problems in racing. He was just a genuine guy. Up until the last time I talked to him, he was still a staunch supporter of the 9:1 compression rule for motors. We'd argue and I'd tell him that motor that once cost $4,000 now cost close to $40,000."

Despite all of Trickle's success, he still always minded his mother. "I remember one day Dick was signing autographs and his mom was in the motorhome and was cooking food for us," said Van Daalwyk. "She told me to tell Richard he had to come in immediately after he signed autographs. He came in as instructed and ate chili before he went out and partied after the fans had left. He always respected his mother."

During one ARTGO show in the mid-1980s, the track received a massive

(Left to right) Darlene Trickle, Sue McKarns, Roger Van Daalwyk, and Dick Trickle celebrate the Trickles' 25th anniversary. (Roger Van Daalwyk collection)

downpour in a very short amount of time.

"Guys were jumping off the guardrail swimming, tires were floating around," said Van Daalwyk. "Dale Earnhardt was scheduled to race that day, but we ended up rescheduling. Earnhardt's car owner, Richard Childress, popped in behind our concession stand. He was a real modest, unassuming guy. He was standing there by himself, basically just trying to get out of the rain. He grabbed some food and we chatted for quite a bit. He was a real nice guy."

The game of marketing and advertising for WIR has changed drastically since the early 1970s.

"Social media might help, but it doesn't get to everybody," said Van Daalwyk. "One thing it is doing is taking away from our local newspapers. We used to take out big display ads in the local papers and the racing trade papers. It listed everything we had going on with pictures in them, too. People could hang onto that and remember the date. We don't have much of that anymore. And social media is partly to blame for that. A lot of people are listening to Sirius radio because they don't want to listen to commercials. I still buy a good amount of radio ads. Am I still reaching everybody? I don't know. We're trying to do a little bit of everything. Television was way too expensive. The price of that has come down. If you don't have the right footage, it doesn't even pay to run ads."

What has been Van Daalwyk's biggest headache in running the race track over the years? Without hesitation he said, "The weather. My dad told me to quit worrying about the weather. You can't change it. I asked him, 'Did you worry about it?' He said, 'Not anymore. That's why I have ulcers now.' You can't change it anyhow. That by far is the biggest problem we face on race day."

Van Daalwyk pointed to the annual Eve of Destruction events held every September as the biggest success story with WIR.

"On most Thursday nights, I can look in the stands where somebody is for the stock car races, they sit in the same place pretty much every week," he said. "On the night of the Eve, I can't do that. Ninety percent of those fans are non- race fans and they just want to see stuff get wrecked. The crowds are huge and bigger than I could have ever imagined."

"With a new high school and high-scale housing creeping near the race track in the 2000s, noise complaints have popped up from time to time.

"We do everything we can to get the races done earlier, preferably by 10 p.m.," he said. "We used to start every night at 8 p.m. Now we start at 6:45. We do try to keep the neighbors happy. WIR is about family. We've got over 100 part-time people working on any given race night – some of whom have been with us for over thirty-five years. There are kids and even folks' grandkids work here. WIR would not be where it is today without the dedication of the friends and family that work here. They sacrifice a lot of their time all season long. WIR is their track."

Van Daalwyk plans on continuing as the owner/operator of WIR until the completion of the 2017 racing season, and then spending more time at his cottage up north.

"I plan on selling the track to my son, Dan, and his wife, Ginger," said Van Daalwyk. "Dan grew up around this, and this way we'll be able to keep the Van Daalwyk tradition of running WIR long into the future."

(Left to right) Bucky Wagner, Roger Paul, Gene Wheeler, Clyde Schumacher (Clyde Schumacher collection)

Clyde Schumacher
Always Smilin'

According to "Smilin' Clyde" Schumacher, KK Sports Arena (later known as Wisconsin International Raceway) originally was built out of spite.

Schumacher, now eighty-six years old, earned the nickname "Smilin' Clyde" for his wide, ear-to-ear smile that never seemed to disappear, no matter what the circumstances of the day or night. The lifelong native of Kimberly was one of the founding fathers of KK Sports Arena. Just how he got to that point is an interesting tale in itself. Schumacher's first race was in 1957 at Gordy's Outagamie Speedway in Apple Creek.

"I had a 1948 Ford four-door sedan and I had fifty dollars invested in it tops," quipped Schumacher. "I was running a filling station on Newberry Street between Kimberly and Appleton. Schmidt Oil owned the station. I was leasing it. One of Schmidt Oil's men, Art Schmidt, stopped in the station one day. He said to me, 'Firestone store is going out of business over on

Wisconsin Avenue. Let's go look that thing over and see if there is anything you'd like to sell here at your service station.' I was going to junk out my Ford at Valley Auto Parts."

Schmidt and Schumacher wound up buying out all of the parts from that Firestone store.

"We put up a big sign that everything was for sale for $1," Schumacher said. "I kept that Ford, and the money we scraped together from that sale helped me turn that Ford into my first race car."

Schumacher was assigned the number 71 by the track scorers. "There were that many cars back then you got assigned a number," he said.

Schumacher credits many of his speed secrets to Alan Pingl, a member of another pit crew. "Alan gave me some tips with setting the points on the distributor and she ran just like a charm after that."

Like many race teams in the late 1950s and 1960s, Schumacher got fast and learned simply by trial and error. "We'd run a fifteen-inch tire on the right rear with forty pounds of air. We'd run a small, seven-inch tire with three pounds of air. We just tinkered with stuff and figured it out after a while."

Early in his career, Schumacher struggled for a bit in the slower first heat before he got to run with the big dogs in the fourth heat, which normally featured the fastest qualifiers of the night. "After a year or so, I finally got fast enough to get into the fourth heat with guys like Bucky Wagner, Bob Wester, and Don and Bob Bennett. Don was Bob's brother. I remember Donny had a rear end from a taxi cab in his racer. And thus, he had a huge advantage for the gearing ratio. It took them three nights before they figured it out. They wanted to DQ him and we gave him credit for being that much smarter than us."

Schumacher took his racer to compete at 141 Speedway in Francis Creek and Oshkosh Raceway before getting involved with KK Sports Arena. "Oshkosh had absolutely huge crowds – I remember that," recalled Schumacher. "You had to be there two hours early to get a seat. It was a very good deal. I set track records there. I got the fast time thing down."

"I was racing Gene Wheeler's car at Oshkosh – it was a Dodge Chrysler product. I got Gene to hold the flag for the national anthem. After the parade lap, we handed off the flag to the pit steward. I took an extra lap afterward at full speed. I about rolled the car and Gene is screaming, 'Slow down, slow down!' That was worth the whole ball of wax."

The fastest car Schumacher ever had was a '56 Pontiac, which was head and shoulders quicker than everyone else for several weeks in the early 1960s. "This was a car owned by Al Piette, and he bought it from some guy in

Wisconsin Rapids," said Schumacher. "We dusted them at Apple Creek bad."

At the end of one night of racing, track officials from the Fox Valley Stock Car Club decided to tear down Schumacher's engine.

"This was late at night. They went to a nearby service station, yanked the motor and decided to pull it apart," Schumacher said. "They thought we were illegal. They popped the manifold and the heads off. They couldn't find anything wrong with the engine. The motor was on the hoist. When they put the motor back in they found a chopped flywheel. It was cut in half to cut the weight down. That was illegal. They barred me from racing there. And that's what prompted me to go and help build KK Sports Arena."

As a result, Schumacher's wife, Joan, and Terry Besaw's wife went up to talk to the club president, Orv Koury.

"They were mad because they were keeping my winning pay from one night earlier. They were tearing us down week after week," Schumacher explained. Koury wound up sending the wives certified letters banning them from coming into the races. Through it all, Clyde kept on smiling.

With no local track to race at, Schumacher took a ride to visit Connie DeLeeuw at some farmland he owned near Highway 55 and KK in Kaukauna. DeLeeuw had the land. Joe Van Daalwyk had the construction company. Schumacher had the racing plan. In 1962, KK Sports Arena was built out of spite. The track consisted of a quarter-mile, dirt oval in its first season.

The crowd seating was built into the hill. Schumacher parted ways with Van Daalwyk and DeLeeuw after just one season. Although Schumacher pulled out of any type of management/ownership role, he continued to race at KK Sports Arena for a few different car owners over the years, including Al Piette, Gene Wheeler and Terry Besaw. Schumacher was the first driver locally to tow his racer on a flatbed-type race hauler.

"That was a pretty big deal back then, because pretty much everyone else hauled their race cars to the track with a tow bar," said Schumacher.

When he wasn't racing upward of four nights a week at times, he also helped raise five kids and even played trombone in a five-piece Dixie band called Bob Gordon's.

"We had a blast over the years racing with the guys," said Schumacher. "Whichever driver got fast time, they had to always buy the first round of drinks for everybody at the saloon afterwards. Then whoever won the feature bought the second round."

After the bars closed, Schumacher would invite everyone to his humble abode in Kimberly. "Heck, those guys would tow their cars and we'd have five or six race cars lined up and down our street. Even though we'd mix it up on the track, we'd party hard and drink beer a lot of times until the sun came up."

Schumacher was one of the best when it came to time trials, often nailing fast time and breaking many track records at ovals across Wisconsin. Races were handicapped in the 1960s, and the fast timer usually had to start from "the back of the bus" in the last row. As such, a driver really earned his feature wins. Other drivers would often sandbag, or intentionally qualify at a slower time, in an effort to land a spot in or near the front row.

"Glen Bessette was a nice guy, but was a terrible sandbagger and everyone knew it," said Schumacher. "I mentioned something to him once and he just laughed about it. So I took extra pride when I'd pass him from the back to beat him."

With his winning ways, Schumacher had fans who were kids but also some ladies as well.

"Women were always sending him letters in the mail with lip prints and perfume on them," said Joan Schumacher, Clyde's wife. "Apparently they didn't know he was a happily married man with five children. We'd both laugh about it."

Joan Schumacher once won a Powder Puff race for women in the 1960s. "The prize for winning the Powder Puff back then was a bottle of wine. Problem was by the time I got off the track, they already had the bottle of wine drank! We had more fun than a barrel of monkeys. It doesn't seem like we ever were home. Looking back I don't know how we did it."

The highlight of Schumacher's career at KK Sports Arena was beating the legendary Dick Trickle in a 50-lap feature in 1968. "They had twin 50s that day," Schumacher recalled. "I won and then crashed out on the second lap of the second 50-lapper."

Schumacher won sixteen out of 18 features on the dirt at Shawano one year. He also scored sixteen clean sweeps in one season, netting fast time and winning both the heat race and main event all on the same night. With his success, Schumacher was sometimes a target from drivers who were hot under the collar during the heat of the battle.

"I recall at Oshkosh one night, one Joe Crass from Maribel came after me," Schumacher chuckled. "He went after me through the back window of my car. But I grabbed him by the neck and told him he wasn't in a real good position to do that."

Compared to the era in which Schumacher found much of his success, the modern era of stock car racing has become very expensive. "It wasn't much different back then – it was all relative," said Schumacher. "I do remember breaking even one year. I always split the prize money with my car owners with a 50/50 split."

Schumacher was out of dough toward the end of his career. "I wasn't even going to race my last year, and I went to my buddy Cliff Wydeven – he was an insurance guy. I told him I didn't have the cash to race. I told him I needed five or six grand just to get a new car built. Cliff opened a drawer, and there were stacks and stacks of 100-dollar bills. Wydeven said, 'Take whatever you need to get your car on the track.' He was a great sponsor."

Following Schumacher's retirement in 1968, JJ Smith took over the number 30 car – the Terry Besaw-owned Ford Torino Schumacher helped prepare. Smith won over thirty features with that racer.

Schumacher's last win was in a Legends race at the then-renamed WIR during the Dixieland Challenge in 1992. He drove Russell Keberlein's sportsman car. "That was a lot of fun, and I can say I won the last ever race I was involved in," he said.

Schumacher has fond memories from his fifteen-year racing career. "The camaraderie was great – we had wonderful friends," he said. "Even though I was a fourth heat guy, I would mingle and talk with the first heat guys. It didn't matter to me. Some of those faster guys thought they were better than others. Not me. We used to stop at Vic's all the time in Bonduel after the races. We'd stop there with the Trudell clan out of Appleton. Just fun times all the way around."

Schumacher was known to bust out his trombone and strike up a few other pals with instruments. "One Saturday night, we all started playing *When the Saints Come Marching In*. We walked out on Main Street and the whole bunch of us paraded into another bar across the street. We just had a blast."

As of this writing, Schumacher remains healthy. His advice? "Keep smiling and don't let this world bother you."

KK Sports Arena Late Model Drivers - 1968

1	Don Kracht	Two Rivers
3	Harvey Aschenbrenner	Fond du Lac
4	Jerry Smith	Appleton
5	Lyle Nabbefeldt	Wisconsin Rapids
5	Tom Van Dreel	West De Pere
6	Jerry Reichenberger	Oshkosh
9	Roger Regeth	Appleton
10	Bob Kempen	Hilbert
12	Hilarien Michlig	Abbotsford
15	Rich Somers	Stevens Point
16	Bill Fitzgerald	Two Rivers
28	Keith Luedtke	Milwaukee
29	Ken Pankratz	Mosinee
30	Clyde Schumacher	Kimberly
31	Bob Marquis	West De Pere
38	Paul Feldner	Colgate
48	Bob Bennett	Greenville
49	Bill Nelson	Minneapolis, Minnesota
50	Gene Marmor	River Grove
57	Robert Dalsky	Wausau
70	Jerry Smith	Medina
80	Bob Schultz	Appleton
90	Stu Nitzke	Berlin
99	Dick Trickle	Wisconsin Rapids

Ron Leek in his usual position at a racetrack with a microphone in his hand. (Laura & Mark Bruederle photo)

Ron Leek
Getting it Started

When KK Sports Arena hosted its inaugural event as a D-shaped, half-mile paved oval Memorial Day weekend of 1968, it was a public relations man from Chicagoland who helped put the shiny, new Kaukauna track on the map on a regional basis – right out of the box. Ron Leek had a background as a drag racing announcer and P.R. magnate in the greater Chicagoland area.

"I was announcing upwards of five to six nights a week at dragstrips between the U.S. and Canada back then," said Leek. "I had some success promoting some of the bigger drag racing events in the mid-1960s."

A mutual business acquaintance of Leek's had done business with Joe Van Daalwyk at KK Sports Arena.

"Ed Rachanski had a booking agency, and he sold race tracks their shows and he did stuff with the drag strip at KK," recalled Leek. "Joe was looking for a GM for the entire facility."

In 1967, KK's track had a half-mile oval, but it was clay. The dragstrip had already been up and running. Having been the general manager of drag strips in Illinois, the prospect of running a facility south of Green Bay, Wisconsin, that featured both oval track racing and drag racing peaked Leek's interest.

"Ed sent me up to meet Van Daalwyk and his wife, Marcy," said Leek. "We met them at a supper club in Combined Locks on a Thursday night. Joe liked his cocktails, so to be sociable, I had a couple of drinks, which I normally didn't do."

Since it was a Thursday night, the trio later headed over to Joe's track.

"I couldn't believe what I was seeing," explained Leek. "I mean, Model A's with flatheads were racing against Chevy coupes with GMC six-cylinders. It was like going back into a time museum. I wasn't sure if I was drunk or if this was reality."

After a meeting with Van Daalwyk, Leek agreed to take the job as GM of KK Sports arena. He and his wife packed their bags and moved into an apartment in Appleton.

"When I met with Van Daalwyk, he basically told me he didn't care what I spent, but that there better be enough cars when we have our first race as a paved track in May of 1968," said Leek. "He made it very clear he did not want to be embarrassed. That really was his biggest concern."

Leek set out to make KK like a "mini-Daytona."

"We had this design in mind with the D shape. We were going to run late model cars. Clean looking cars that looked just like what raced at Daytona. That was our goal," said Leek. "I hooked up with Van Daalwyk's brother-in-law, (local race car owner) Al Piette. He was associated with Gene Wheeler. We all came up with this idea about having the cars just sparkle, real full-sized, late model cars."

Crews worked through the winter to pave the oval and pour the concrete walls around the track.

"I remember being out there pouring concrete when it was 10 below zero," said Leek. "It was unreal."

Leek launched an ultra-aggressive public relations and marketing campaign, flooding the local media with frequent releases relating to the status of Wisconsin's newest paved oval.

"I recall doing a lot of stuff with the *Appleton Post-Crescent*," recalled Leek. "I called Al Sampson from TV-11 in Green Bay. He got me some NASCAR footage from a colleague of his at a television station in Charlotte. We put a TV commercial together with that footage. Al was a great guy."

The whole goal with the KK Sports Arena was that a "whole new way of stock car racing" was going to hit Northeast Wisconsin – and in a big way.

"Ron Leek was great at what he did," said Roger Van Daalwyk, Joe's son. "I remember I was a young teenager. I rode with him in this souped-up 1968 Dodge Charger with a hemi in it. We went to Wisconsin Rapids to meet Dick (Trickle) and his wife, Darlene. The reason for the visit was to hammer out a long term agreement to keep Dick Trickle coming to WIR on a regular basis. I remember Dick building his race cars out of a barn back then."

The process of actually recruiting drivers was actively underway.

"I remember hooking up with Dick Trickle and we drove in snow storms to places like Wausau to meet with Dave Marcis, and he totally bought into what we were going to do at KK," said Leek. "Dick (Trickle) was such an awesome man and a great ambassador for the sport. Dick introduced me to Tom Reffner of Rudolph and other people around Wisconsin."

Other Wisconsin drivers built cars to race at the state's newest track, including Rich Somers of Stevens Point, "Smilin' Clyde" Schumacher of Kimberly, Appleton's Milo Van Oudenhoven, Greenville's Bobby Bennett, Marlin Walbeck from Eau Claire, Jim Sauter from Necedah, George Giesen of Menasha, Norm Nelson from Racine, and Roger "The Bear" Regeth of Kimberly.

"Once word got out that we were going to pay $7,500 to win for that first event, we also had some hitters commit to our program from Illinois like Gene Marmor," said Leek. "We had an Iowa contingent of drivers who were coming up from Keokuk, Iowa, like Ernie Derr, Ramo Stott and Don White.

The Blankenships from Iowa were coming up, too."

When word got out across the Midwest that this brand spanking new facility would be shelling out a whopping payout in its inaugural lid-lifter, it drew the attention of officials from USAC, which was as big as NASCAR back then. In the 1960s and into the 1970s, USAC was very territorial about what it perceived to be "their" drivers.

"Derr, Stott, White and Nelson, Regeth and Giesen were all USAC regulars, and they called and were upset that we were going to pay that much money to win a non-sanctioned USAC race," said Leek. "They started threatening some of their regulars, telling them they'd be suspended if they came to our show, which wasn't sanctioned. It was a very risky thing for us at the time, looking back on it, to pay out that kind of money, especially at a track's first-ever race. It was a sizeable gamble."

As the weeks drew closer to the scheduled opener on Memorial Day weekend 1968, Leek was confident he'd have enough cars on hand. But would enough race fans show up to support paying that whopper of a driver payout? "We had some snow the Wednesday before that event in May and (Joe) was starting to get scared," said Leek.

Despite the obstacles, Leek kept his nose to the grindstone. He advertised in a five-state area, including Minnesota, Illinois, Michigan, Indiana and Wisconsin.

"We did stuff with *Hawkeye Racing News* out of Iowa, and did stuff in *Midwest* and *Checkered Flag Racing News,* too," said Leek. "With the local coverage, we were flooding the local newspapers, the radio and TV ads, there wasn't a whole lot more we could have done."

When race day arrived, a stout field of forty drivers representing five states was on hand. The local TV stations were there to cover it.

"Keith Knaack from *Hawkeye Racing News* came up, as did Hugh Deery from Rockford Speedway and Sam Bartus, who went on to build a race track in Madison," said Leek.

When it was all said and done, the race cars were loaded on the haulers, and the track crews began cleaning up, a standing room only crowd of 13,640 fans had attended the inaugural paved track race at KK Sports Arena.

"The gamble paid off and Joe told me later more than once just how much money he made that weekend," said Leek. "He told me after the races that day to come and see him in his office the next day. I figured I would be getting a bonus of some sort for helping bring that many cars and fans to the track."

Well, that bonus never appeared.

"Joe was almost like a larger-than-life type character who could have been from Texas or something," said Leek. "He would go game hunting all over the world. Schools would go through his house on tour and stuff."

Leek would finish out the inaugural season in 1968.

"Our weekly show continued to draw guys from all over," recalled Leek. "The villain back then, no doubt, was Roger Regeth. One Thursday he got into a tangle with (George) Giesen. The fans got riled up. The following week, because of that incident, we had another 600 paid adults in attendance. Word-of-mouth was our best form of advertisement."

After the 1968 season finished up, Leek returned to the Chicago area where he would resume his career as a promoter and announcer of drag racing events across the Midwest. In the off season from drag racing, Leek would drive dump truck. Years later, he would build a trucking company that remains in operation to this day.

"I guess I had to leave KK at the time because Joe (Van Daalwyk) made out like a burglar in that first race and I could just see no future in me working for him any longer," said Leek. "I never burned a bridge, and in fact Joe called me many years later. Our paths had crossed in drag racing. He said to me, 'I knew you were a good promoter, but I didn't realize you were such a good businessman, too,' once he learned about my trucking company."

Leek's role in getting the paved track at KK Sports Arena up and running featured the successful transformation from the coupes to the late models.

"It was fun when I look back," he said. "I had some good memories up there, even though my stay up there was brief."

WIR publicity director Gary Vercauteren (left) in his element with track legend Dick Trickle. (Bob Bergeron photo)

Gary Vercauteren
For Immediate Release

Editor's note: Gary Vercauteren handles publicity for the Wisconsin International Raceway speed complex, handling both the oval track and drag strip activities. A race fan since his youth, Gary grew up across the street from the De Pere Fairgrounds. Vercauteren is the owner of Vercauteren Publishing in Chilton, Wisconsin. This article appeared in the Appleton Post-Crescent *in the 1980s.*

WIR – Joe's Challenge

By Gary Vercauteren

It was a cold March evening in 1972. The snow had begun to melt, but winter was reluctantly losing its grip.

I rang the doorbell and a 50-year-old man opened the door while talking on the telephone, stretching the cord to reach the door knob.

He looked at me quickly and said, "You must be Gary What's His Name."

His attention returned to the phone. "I'm not paying that ----- high rate and you know it. I got somebody in my office. If you've got a better price, call me back." With that, Joe Van Daalwyk hung up the phone, took a couple of puffs on his cigar and looked back at me.

"Take off your coat and sit down," he said.

I knew he was in charge right off the bat. He quickly outlined the history of his race track – Wisconsin International Raceway. Most of it was familiar to me. I had attended nearly every race at the track for the past several seasons and knew that Joe was trying to rebuild a financially troubled and later bankrupt KK Sports Arena.

Track manager Ted Schmalz arrived later and we discussed putting together a late model stock car series for Wisconsin drivers.

"Those USAC boys are just a big pain in the ---," Van Daalwyk said. "I think they'll dry up in a couple of years. That's why we've got to do something different."

Joe was right. The USAC stock car division is no more and his Red, White and Blue State Championship Series is thriving.

An idea became a reality that year in spite of the fact that dirt track racing was drawing big crowds at fairground speedways in Shawano, De Pere, Oshkosh and Seymour.

Dick Trickle, driving a 1970 Mustang, won the first race in the series on a perfect, sunny afternoon. He went to the outside of John Rank on the 26th lap and won by three car lengths. Trickle, of Wisconsin Rapids, went on to establish a national feature win record of 67 victories that year.

A crowd of 7,832 viewed the first race as some 52 cars competed on the half-mile paved oval. Madison's John Ziegler established a new one-lap track record of 21.74 during time trials.

And, Joe was pleased. He even smiled. After all it was his first profitable stock car race since taking over the track in 1971. Several USAC events were large financial losers.

Schmalz released a statement to the press the following week canceling a remaining USAC stock car event.

"We're dropping USAC in favor of our Red, White and Blue state championship," Schmalz said. "The fact that Dick Trickle was not in the lineup for our first USAC race this year cut our attendance in half."

"USAC doesn't have enough races on its schedule to allow any of the good drivers to make a living," he added.

Perhaps the most famous statement came when Schmalz said, "You can't sell a $6.00 show when there's a better one down the street for $3.00."

Schmalz's statements were of course all carefully orchestrated by Van Daalwyk. Joe pulled the strings. He ran the race track. Smoking his cigars, he spent long hours in his office.

There were many long meetings. Hours and hours were spent discussing rules, payoffs and promotions. Joe was a successful businessman. His construction, real estate and restaurant firms were all making big money.

The raceway was perhaps his biggest challenge. It was dead and he revived it. He loved every minute of it, from screaming at radio station owners for running ads after the races had been run to watching his traditional booming fireworks at the start of every race.

The Red, White and Blue series was the start of the turnaround.

In 1975 Joe joined forces with the Fox River Racing Club to promote weekly races at Kaukauna. The drivers raced for 100 percent of the ticket sales for the first full season to get the thing rolling.

It wasn't easy.

At the first meeting, one of the car owners said, "100 percent of nothing is nothing. Ain't it?" Joe heard about the comment and fumed for a couple of days. "What does that son-of-a- ------ think? I've got a million bucks sunk in that place out there," he steamed.

A few days later he settled down and a deal was signed with the Fox River Racing Club.

Today the Kaukauna raceway is considered one of the most successful short tracks in the nation. It's unique design was Joe's idea. He wasn't one to copy someone else. His ideas were originals.

There were times when he'd talk to Hugh Deery, of the Rockford Speedway, over the phone. Most of the talk centered around selling popcorn, hot dogs and beer.

They both had something in common. They were both originals and will never be duplicated.

Joe passed away in 1984, but the sounds of racing engines roaring will continue at his track. He left the world having conquered his biggest challenge.

Dick Trickle poses with his racer in 1976. Trickle was a huge draw for the Red, White and Blue State Championship Series at WIR. (Pete Vercauteren photo)

Red, White and Blue State Championship Series

When the Red, White and Blue State Championship Series was created by Joe Van Daalwyk and Gary Vercauteren in 1972, the series meant different things to different drivers. The series carried with it a lot of prestige in the racing community. It drew Dick Trickle to Wisconsin International Raceway for all of those series races throughout the 1970s and into the 1980s.

"It was truly a who's who on those Sunday afternoons there," said Milton's Dave Watson, a three-time RW&B champion. "When you had all these heavy hitters from different tracks in the state, it was a big deal. I was only racing for a couple of years when I came home from Vietnam."

Watson won his first title in 1973 and would go on to win the Fox River Racing Club's Thursday's night title in 1982.

"Dick (Trickle) was running it and Joe Shear was my teammate for those early years and he was tough," said Watson. "Then you factor in the other Central Wisconsin guys like (Tom) Reffner, (Marv) Marzofka, (Jimmy) Back and later on Larry Detjens. Personally, I really liked WIR because it was different and not a cookie-cutter track."

Watson teamed up with Beloit's Shear, a future four-time RW&B

champion, in the early 1970s.

"I bought Joe's car in 1970 and we raced out of the same garage for four years," recalled Watson. "Joe was a very quiet guy. He was pretty intense and he was pretty shy. If they didn't know him, they thought he was aloof. But that wasn't really the case. Truth is he was thinking about racing all the time. Joe was a good man."

Shear won RW&B titles in 1979, 1987, 1988 and 1996. He died of cancer March 6, 1998.

The RW&B series garnered miles and miles of ad copy in the regional racing papers *Midwest Racing News* and *Checkered Flag Racing News*. Gary Vercauteren, WIR's P.R. man at the time, was one of the best in the racing biz.

"Gary Vercauteren was great at what he did and he lived and breathed racing," said Watson. "He really promoted the Red, White and Blue series hard. He got the drivers there. And then it was hyped up. It seemed most of the race fans in Wisconsin knew about those shows and that series when it started."

Watson was almost always a hired gun throughout his career and landed top-notch rides.

"I remember I drove for Lyle Lundy when I won the Thursday night title in '82," recalled Watson. "Lyle was from Waukesha. He had a tire shop. He was into advertising. We both got turned onto each other from Mike Randerson. Mike was an absolute genius. I couldn't (race) today. If you don't have an uncle or a grandpa with a big checkbook, it's pretty tough to do. I was lucky enough to basically race for a living. WIR had the three series specials, plus the spring opener and the fall special they had. Those were five races every year that paid real well."

***

It was cold, hard cash that drew a pair of Central Wisconsin's finest to the Red White and Blue – Rudolph's Tom Reffner and Nekoosa's "Marvelous Marv" Marzofka. Reffner dominated the asphalt short track scene in the mid-1970s at the height of his racing career.

"The Blue Knight," as he was affectionately known, won an incredible sixty-seven feature races in 1975, racing his tricked-out AMC Javelin. "We won 65 percent of the races we entered that year," said Reffner, who also pocketed $50,000 in prize money in 1975. Not bad for a pipefitter by trade!

Reffner met his good friend Trickle for the first time while they participated in Boy Scouts. Reffner was just eight years old. Before the Central Wisconsin Racing Association was formed, Reffner and his pals would traipse across the state racing four, sometimes five nights a week. Reffner honed his craft, winning frequently in the 1970s at tracks such as Plover, Capital Speedway in Madison, Dells Motor Speedway, State Park Speedway in Rib Mountain and La Crosse Fairgrounds Speedway.

"We started running WIR after they blacktopped it in the late 1960s," said Reffner. "That was the first year they ran the USAC-type cars. Jim Back and I were together at that time. We owned a car then. When they started running regular late models on Thursday nights, we came over to run there for a while.

"WIR was real similar with the gearing to West Salem (La Crosse). We had experience on the longer track. WIR and La Crosse are really close except for the dogleg. As far as the track went, it wasn't a big deal. We had gearing and such. That bigger track drew us. They are both horsepower tracks. WIR is tough on the brakes – later in the longer races anyways."

Reffner was always a frontrunner in the RW&B, winning some of those feature races. But for some reason, fate would have it where "The Blue Knight" would get snake-bitten and always seemed to come up short.

"I should have won two or three of those Red, White and Blues," said Reffner. "I got second a few times in the series and won some features there. Something always seemed to happen with crashes and blown motors along the way."

Reffner played bridesmaid roles three different times in the RW&B in Kaukauna despite winning a number of those series feature races. Drivers and their crews would change gears on Sundays at the track (if they weren't too hot) and boogie over to Golden Sands Speedway in Plover.

"Heck, those few Sundays were hectic," recalled Reffner. "I remember a lot of times we wouldn't even wait to get paid. We'd just hit the road and change gears when we got to the track."

It wasn't all peaches and cream for Reffner at WIR. "I had a few bad wrecks along the way," he said. "I remember getting into it with Larry Schuler one time on the backstretch. It was a bad crash. A real bad one."

The SuperAmerica sponsorship deal in the 1970s also helped boost Reffner and Trickle's popularity.

"John Boegeman was from Shakopee, Minnesota, and he was the first guy they sponsored," said Reffner. "He was the Black Knight. He was real good friends with their advertising manager. I was sharing a race shop with Dick (Trickle) back then. They sponsored Dick after Johnny. Then they picked me up and I was the Purple Knight. Dick was the White Knight. The sponsorship actually started back in 1973. I only had a small sticker in '74 and my bigger deal came in '75."

It wasn't that much money involved early on, "but what they really helped with was the fuel for the hauler," said Reffner. "There was some money we got, but that free fuel to go to the tracks was huge, as much as we were running. That made traveling that much easier to do."

SuperAmerica would help with engine and chassis purchases for the teams during later years as well.

With the brutal travel schedule, Reffner relied heavily on crew chief Pete Haferman and crew member John Bovee during the five-nights-a-week grind.

"They'd drive to the track and back home from the track while I slept," said Reffner. "It was the only time I could really sleep. I was a pipefitter by trade. When it got real busy with racing, I'd slow down with the work. I remember one year we ran 120 races."

Reffner's wife, DeeDee, would often serve as his lone pit crew member in the later years of his career.

***

Marv Marzofka made WIR a weekly stop one entire season.

"They were paying so well it was a pretty easy decision to come over there," said Marzofka. "I had been running the Dells and had sponsors there. I butted heads with ol' Roger Regeth there for a while. We pretty much had things our way. You could walk out of there with between $700 and $1,000 with the big cars. The pay was incredible back then compared to what promoters in Central Wisconsin were paying out.

"Then when they started the Red, White and Blue series, we'd come back for those shows. (Jimmy) Back and Trickle bought a car and wanted me to drive it. I had sold my car. I was a top-five car. I never won a race in the series, but I had a bunch of top-five finishes. I'd like to say I was always a frontrunner. Trickle wouldn't let anybody else win those – he dominated at WIR."

Sundays were a busy day of hustle and bustle, as the crew would quickly load up and hurry back to race Sunday evening closer to home at Plover.

"We had to know where the police were sitting on that drive back on Highway 54," Marzofka quipped. "I never had a bad wreck at WIR. It wasn't that hard to drive. It was hell on motors though, because we had the tight corners and the long straightaways. If you wanted to power out of the corners, the tongue of the engine was hanging out by the end. She was usually tired.

"One month, we ran seventeen days in a row. Monday was Queens' Day for the wives. We hit Marne, Michigan, and Cayuga, Canada, Monday and Tuesday. Wednesday was La Crosse, Thursday Wausau, Friday Dells, Saturday Madison, and Sundays Plover. Then we'd start all over again by throwing in another special out of state, and it was like a marathon.

"I'd take an hour or two of vacation at a clip so we could go racing so much. I ran Elko, Minnesota, weekly one year because I had Iten Chevrolet from Minnesota as a sponsor. I'm catching up now on the sleep we missed. In addition to the great payout, I remember those Sunday afternoons being very, very hot at WIR. But great times all around."

Marzofka is now 76 years old, and like Reffner, devotes much of his time to the Dick Trickle Memorial project based in Wisconsin Rapids.

Red, White and Blue State Champions

1972 – Dick Trickle
1973 – Dave Watson
1974 – Rich Somers
1975 – Johnny Ziegler
1976 – Dave Watson
1977 – Dick Trickle
1978 – Dick Trickle
1979 – Joe Shear
1980 – Dick Trickle
1981 – Dick Trickle
1982 – Dave Watson
1983 – Dick Trickle
1984 – Dick Trickle
1985 – Mark Martin
1986 – Mark Martin
1987 – Joe Shear
1988 – Joe Shear
1989 – Doug Herbst
1990 – Rich Bickle Jr.
1991 – Jim Weber
1992 – Robbie Reiser
1993 – Robbie Reiser
1994 – Steve Carlson/Jim Weber
1995 – Matt Kenseth
1996 – Joe Shear
1997 – Jim Weber
1998 – Rod Wheeler
1999 – Lowell Bennett
2000 – Rod Wheeler
2001 – Terry Baldry
2002 – Terry Baldry
2003 – Jeff Van Oudenhoven
2004 – Lowell Bennett
2005 – Jeff Van Oudenhoven
2006 – Mike Gardner
2007 – Gregg Haese
2008 – Tim Rothe
2009 – Lowell Bennett
2010 – Lowell Bennett
2011 – Ross Kenseth
2012 – Lowell Bennett
2013 – Jeff Van Oudenhoven
2014 – Brett Piontek/Maxwell Schultz
2015 – Steve Apel
2016 – Casey Johnson
2017 – Bobby Kendall
2018 – Bobby Kendall
2019 – Maxwell Schultz
2020 – Jesse Oudenhoven

Victor Getzloff (left) served as crew chief for three of the seven Red, White and Blue state championships won by Dick Trickle (right). (Bob Bergeron photo)

Victor Getzloff and Dick Trickle
Life of the Party

Editor's note: Dick Trickle, one of the country's winningest short track drivers, died May 16, 2013, from an apparent self-inflicted gunshot wound. The incident occurred at a cemetery in Boger City, North Carolina. Trickle had been dealing with chronic pain for years and saw many doctors – none of whom could find the source of his pain.

Victor Getzloff and his brother, Albert, were hitchhiking to the races at the track in Adams-Friendship near their rural Bancroft home in Central Wisconsin in the late 1950s. Just twelve years old at the time, the brothers were picked up by a man who was en route to the track – with a race car tugging behind a pickup truck with a not-so-sturdy-looking tow chain.

"Hop in guys," said the stranger. The Getzloff boys climbed inside the race car that was being towed. They were just happy to get a lift to the races.

Little did Albert know that the man who was picking them up, Richard

Trickle, would eventually team up with "Big Vic" as his crew chief years later and form one of the most dominant teams in the history of short track racing in the United States.

"Dick was seven years older than us when he first picked us up that day," recalled Vic Getzloff, now sixty-eight. "We basically wound up being on his pit crew sort like a trial-by-fire."

Trickle would go on to win an incredible sixty-seven feature races in 1972. Conservative estimates have Trickle winning close to 1,200 short track races in his storied career. His wins were legendary. Over the years, nobody got to know Trickle as well as his crew chief.

"Albert and I were the tire dealers for the Central Wisconsin Racing Association (CWRA)," Getzloff said. "He bought a lot of tires from us in the beginning. He'd pick through all of them. He knew around the twenty-second week of the year – usually in April – that's when the best tires were produced. He'd buy a bunch of those McCreary tires."

When The Getzloff brothers weren't selling tires, they were racing themselves on the CWRA circuit.

"I had a race car I wrecked pretty good in '81 and Dick gave me one of his to race," said Getzloff. "Dick asked me to go work for him as his crew chief, but I had to quit racing myself. So I did."

The rest, as they say, is history. Trickle would go on to win seven Red,

Dick Trickle in 1973. (Pete Vercauteren photo)

White and Blue titles at Wisconsin International Raceway. That feat has never been matched by any other driver to this day. Getzloff was crew chief for three of those titles in the 1980s.

"WIR was a real good track to us," said Getzloff. "And to top it off, the Red, White and Blue was a good-paying deal. To win that was a big deal for the prestige, too."

One Sunday afternoon at WIR, Trickle had a scary moment.

"His steering wheel popped right off on the last lap of the trophy dash," Getzloff chuckled. "The spindle had come off. He gripped the shaft around it and somehow managed to keep the car off the wall. Not many guys could have pulled that off – but Dick did. We loved WIR. We had some great battles with Sauter, Shear, Tom (Reffner), and locally they had JJ Smith. Roger (Van Daalwyk) really took care of us there. We had some great times at Kaukauna."

The team gave the race cars in their stable colorful names.

"We decided to name the cars after the characters from *Gunsmoke*," said Getzloff. "We had Miss Kitty, Matt Dillion and Alexis. We named our hauler Ruth. That was the name of Festus' mule on the show."

For as often as Trickle raced – often more than 100 short track shows a year – his equipment was always looking sharp, even into the dog days of the season late in the year.

"Dick always said when it came to the race car, we dressed up like we were going to a ball."

Over the years, Trickle gained a reputation for rolling into the track at the last minute. Stories of them unloading number 99 without as much as any warmup laps and breaking the track record at any track were pretty common.

"A lot of people said we were doing that on purpose, that we were doing it to avoid tech or whatever, but that wasn't the case," explained Getzloff. "We had that car in the shop and scaled it, and we wanted that thing ready to go when we unloaded. We were always ready."

Getzloff earned "Crew Chief of the Year" honors in the American Speed Association (ASA) circuit in 1984 and 1985. With two sets of race cars, the team utilized a private airplane to jet Trickle and crew across the Midwest.

"We'd run Michigan on a Friday or Saturday, and we'd fly to WIR some Sundays on that plane," said Getzloff.

Getzloff's first time flying featured Trickle's pilot, Neil Jacobs, crash

Dick Trickle was WIR's version of a rock star. (www.danlewisphoto.net)

landing on WIR's dragstrip. All involved escaped unhurt.

"One thing about Dick Trickle most people don't know was that he was great at helping out new drivers," said Green Bay native Scott Hansen. "When I decided to go racing full time on the asphalt, Dick invited me and my crew out to his shop in Wisconsin Rapids. We were all surprised at all of the information he gave us. He provided so many pointers. His attitude about that was, 'I'd rather have you running well and not be a hazard.'"

A little-known fact about Trickle was that he possessed amazing upper body strength.

"He did some boxing and stuff in high school," said Getzloff. "And years ago, he really had to horse those cars around without any power steering. So his arms were big and he was really, really strong. He didn't have a lot of motor either in the early years. So he really worked on the chassis a lot. He won with his chassis tuning."

Moose Peterson was a race car owner who owned a car dealership.

"Moose used to always arm wrestle his drivers," said Getzloff. "Dick beat every one of his guys. He was that strong. I'd never seen him get beat in an arm wrestling match."

Trickle also acquired a reputation as a man who loved to work hard and play even harder.

"Dick was a funny guy and he loved to have a few laughs," said Getzloff. "But a lot of that perception he had was blown out of proportion. He liked to have a few beers. But there were a lot of half-drank beers around there. We installed a cigarette lighter in the car. Then the legend grew. It was something to talk about for his fans and promoters."

"Dick helped a lot of drivers out over the years," Getzloff continued. "It was a fun time. He was the best with the fans. He always signed autographs. He would stay lined up for hours. A lot of those other drivers wouldn't stick around, but Dick always would."

Among the biggest paydays Getzloff ever helped Trickle earn was winning the $50,000 World Crown 300 at Georgia International Speedway in 1983.

"Dick got a crown and a cape for that big win," said Getzloff. "It was the biggest paying race he ever won. There weren't a lot of people there because the weather was rainy. The promoter took it in the shorts that day, but he paid us out in full."

These days, Getzloff is semi-retired.

"I do help out Johnny Sauter with his NASCAR truck gig once in a while, and I drive his hauler around for his short track car," said Getzloff. "I also worked with Tim Sauter for a while in the ASA championship. I did tires for both of those guys."

Getzloff has seen significant changes with short track racing in the Midwest.

"You can't get any cars anymore," said Getzloff. "The money isn't there. The fans can't afford to go. They got high dollar motors and stuff. Getting to and from the race track got a lot more expensive too."

As for his memories of Trickle?

"I lost my dad in 1958," he said. "So Dick really was like a father figure to me."

A young Mark Martin poses with his car in 1980. (Pete Vercauteren photo)

Mark Martin
Fast out of the Box

Mark Martin, a NASCAR Hall of Fame Class of 2017 inductee, never met a race track he didn't like.

The Batesville, Arkansas, native was a two-time Red, White and Blue state champion at Wisconsin International Raceway, driving for Jerry Gunderman of Milwaukee. Martin had come back to the Midwest and raced short track specials, ASA and ARTGO series events after attempting to run Winston Cup down south on his own dime from 1981 to 1983.

"I think the first time I ran WIR was likely one of those ARTGO shows, probably around 1978," recalled Martin. "I loved that place. I remember going into turn one it was sort of uphill. Then when you go around three and four, I remember that inside guardrail and the front straightaway had a unique shape to it. It was a cool place and it was real unique as how you had to drive that track. I went to a lot of short tracks around the country, but WIR was one of a kind."

Martin honed his craft running many Wisconsin tracks, including WIR.

"I ran all the ARTGO shows I could, and for a while, I'd pick and choose the bigger races," said Martin. "Wisconsin racing was very, very instrumental in my racing career in general. It prepared me to have the type of driver etiquette that those guys helped mold me into in the late '70s and early to mid-'80s."

Martin took full advantage during an era where a driver could run four or sometimes five nights a week.

"There were times you could race six nights a week and even twice on Sundays," quipped Martin. "That seat time made everybody better back then."

Of all the drivers Martin went wheel-to-wheel with at WIR, he thoroughly enjoyed running with the pride of Wisconsin Rapids, Dick Trickle.

"Dick was a true sportsman. He raced hard and wanted to win," said Martin. "But he was very fair and he was helpful even though I was competition to him. He took pride in his operation, and ultimately he helped mold and shape the way I raced and the code I lived by both on and off the track. I have all the respect in the world for Wisconsin short track drivers. Running up at WIR was a great experience for me and I learned a lot along the way."

Bob Abitz was a driver himself before concentrating on the tech inspection side of the racing business. (Pete Vercauteren photo)

Bob Abitz
The Flyin' School Teacher

Bob Abitz has been fortunate enough to play the short track racing game on both sides of the fence as a driver and a tech official. What's even more amazing is he acted as both a driver and tech inspector at the same time for some years, which is almost unheard of in modern times.

"The Flyin' School Teacher" taught collision repair and other automotive specialties as a shop teacher at Freedom High School.

"The district hired me in 1972," recalled Abitz, who was also a racer at the time. "I began racing at WIR that same year with a Plymouth Roadrunner. I'd race for those first Red, White and Blue shows we had."

As a shop teacher, Abitz exposed his students to many different disciplines in the automotive industry. They would rebuild engines. They went to frame shops in the area and learned how to fix cars.

"I've had students I've taken under my wing and a lot of them served on my pit crew along the way," said Abitz. "I had some kids who had not been out of Outagamie County. They got to go with me to races all over the Midwest, including Illinois and Indiana. For them, racing was an extension of the school. I never had any beer with us, either. Just soda."

Abitz was asked by Wisconsin International Raceway owner Joe Van Daalwyk to write the rules for the Red, White and Blue State Championship series when it was created in 1972.

"Joe says to me one day, 'I've got to find you a sponsor,'" said Abitz. "He came to me and said, 'I've got Old Style beer to sponsor your race car. It's a $5,000 deal.'"

As a high school teacher, there was no way Abitz could take that sponsor money from a brewer – which was a whopping amount for that time period. Abitz refused to take a dime.

"I think for that reason, Joe just thought the world of me after that," said Abitz. "Every other driver would have jumped at the chance."

Old Style would appear years later as a sponsor on cars driven by Jim Sauter and Rod Wheeler.

WIR was struggling to get late models on the track in the early to mid-1970s. One of the reasons was many other paved tracks in the state had their own individual wrinkles in their respective rulebooks which discouraged drivers from other tracks to tow to Kaukauna.

"I remember Rich Somers from Stevens Point and I were two of the very few late model drivers who made it to WIR every Thursday night that year," said Abitz. "That year, the rules in Wisconsin you could have called them 'every which way but close.'"

Clem Droste was president of Central Wisconsin Racing Association (CWRA), which sanctioned races at tracks located in Wausau, Madison, Wisconsin Dells and La Crosse.

"Sunday was always open for specials that year, and theoretically you could race six of the seven days of the week with the specials," Abitz pointed out. "In '75, we were starting to draw guys like Larry Schuler and Roger Regeth to WIR on a weekly basis. That was the type of caliber of cars that started coming there weekly."

Talk of rules changes began to surface when the post-season meetings commenced in the fall.

"There were a lot of leftover guys from the Apple Creek days with their cars, and I suggested we needed to change our rules to adapt to other tracks," said Abitz. "A few guys asked why. The answer was simple. So we can race someplace else if you do want to chase other tracks."

Roger "The Bear" Regeth stood up at one of the meetings.

"He said, 'Abitz, why don't you start writing the rules?' Clem and I got together and started to blend the rules with CWRA," said Abitz. "I even got Slinger to go with it sort of. Lake Geneva was also interested in what we were doing at the time."

Different tracks ran different tires in 1977 and 1978. McCreary, Firestone and Hoosiers were tire brands run by different ovals.

"By '78, we had a uniform tire rule in Wisconsin," Abitz proclaimed. "You could go anyplace and run the same tire. Before that, I had to have a three-tire rack to go race elsewhere because of all the different tire options we had. It was crazy."

The process of blending the rules with other tracks took some legwork.

"Chuck Ippolitto, Jim Salentine and I would make trips over to Adams-Friendship in Central Wisconsin to go to those CWRA meetings," said Abitz. "We'd see what they were doing and then we'd have our meeting and decide what we were going to do."

Abitz was in Joe Van Daalwyk's good graces, putting him in position to suggest that Van Daalwyk start running a fall special. With the weekly racing done at most Wisconsin tracks, he reasoned it would draw drivers from several Wisconsin and Midwestern tracks.

"We started running those races after that," said Abitz. "But those bigger specials sometimes didn't come without their problems as far as tech inspecting."

Meanwhile, Abitz was experiencing some sour luck with his own racing program.

"I raced on a budget and was doing engine rebuilds in the winter time for money," said Abitz. "I had 'x' amount of money I spent on racing for the full season and we stopped when the money ran out."

In 1982, Abitz was at seven blown motors with two different engine builders by July 1.

"I said that's it, we're done," he said.

Mike Lemke would assist Abitz in getting another motor together. When the final checkered flag flew in 1982, Abitz's race car had chewed up and spit out a total of nine engines. Lemke would start assisting Abitz with inspecting cars – "teching" is the term – and continues to do that to this day.

Abitz's teching duties occasionally created awkward situations when he was still racing the Red, White and Blue races, especially if there was an issue with a car that finished in front of him.

"Bill Oas was a driver from Minnesota who was running the Red, White and Blue series in 1982," Abitz recalled. "One of the Bilstein shock absorbers that he was running were only allowed in ARTGO. We said you couldn't run them for a weekly show to keep the cost down. I missed the feature and I'm coming up to the semi-feature. He's gliding through the corners. I'm bouncing through the corners. I'm studying the car. When we got to tech after the races, we discovered he had the silver Bilstein shocks. I went and got Dick Trickle and told Dick, 'You have to disqualify him because he's got illegal shocks.' I couldn't do it, obviously, because I finished one spot behind him. He got the transfer spot until he was disqualified. So I wound up getting the transfer spot instead of Oas. That's why I had to call Trickle over to be impartial."

Oas learned an important lesson that when you travel to an unfamiliar track, the first thing you should do is run your car over the track scales. Always run across the scales and always know what the rules are.

"Truthfully, it was a very hard thing to do, both tech cars and race," said Abitz. "These front-running guys are running across the scales. I could see all of their percentages they were running, which is really key to knowing what their hot setups were. They had confidence in me so I could ride both sides of the fence."

Abitz hung up his racing helmet in 1983 and devoted his full attention to becoming a tech inspector. It wasn't long before he was handling the tech chores at other venues as well as WIR.

"After I sold all of my own racing equipment, I got calls from John McKarns from ARTGO and Donn Oliver, who was the president of Norway (Michigan) Speedway," said Abitz. "Both wanted me to work for them, and I did."

It didn't take long and Wayne Erickson from Slinger Speedway was calling, also soliciting Abitz and his skills. Abitz has his share of tales about catching drivers trying to sneak one by the "Flying School Teacher." (Abitz's nickname)

"I remember one night I saw Augie Derenne get his car towed off on the hook after a bad wreck," said Abitz. "I saw he had an aluminum block motor in it. I told Augie, 'You know when you get this thing fixed, you really should get rid of that aluminum block motor.'"

Or the time a Red, White and Blue race was red-flagged because of a rain delay.

"The cars are all parked on the track and no crew members are supposed to be out there," explained Abitz. "All of a sudden, I look toward Scott Hansen's car. It looks like the car is moving a bit. I look at his car and Richie Wauters (NASCAR truck owner and Hansen crew chief at the time) is underneath the car trying to adjust the coil over shocks. That was a big no-no."

One night, Waupaca's Tom Haen got caught not once, but twice in the same night with an illegal carburetor.

"Tom looked exceptionally fast that night, much faster than he was normally running, so I looked under the hood and we got him once," said Abitz. "Sure enough, he bolted another illegal carb the next time out. We got him again."

Carburetors were the place where crew chiefs like Wauters liked playing the cat and mouse game most.

"Guys like Richie keep us on our toes," admitted Abitz. "Richie and I are still friends. The drivers said if we had a disagreement one day, the next day it would be a clean slate. Every day is a new day. I still try to live by that."

Abitz would later work for NASCAR in the ReMax Challenge series.

"Looking back over the years with things like the 9:1 compression rule we implemented, to me it kept a level playing field," said Abitz. "That was my big thing. We tried to keep the rules in check so the little guy at Kaukauna could compete with the Scott Hansens and the Terry Baldrys. So when they rolled out, at least they knew they had a chance to win."

Rene Grode displays one of his scrapbooks in his Black Creek, Wisconsin, home. (Joe Verdegan photo)

Rene Grode
Beating the Bushes

Although his title read "Fox River Racing Club president," Rene Grode felt like a college recruiter most of the time during the mid- to late 1970s.

Grode was one of the founding fathers of the FRRC and promoted the Thursday night races as secretary and president. With Wisconsin International Raceway reopening, Grode and the club's officers were in an ongoing effort to lure drivers from neighboring dirt tracks. Grode was constantly beating the bushes, attending races several nights a week to try and get drivers to the pavement on Thursday nights.

"I would make deals with guys like Gary Roehborn or Cliff Ebben who were on the fence about trying it out on the tar," recalled Grode. "I'd buy these runoff asphalt tires from the teams that were running, as many of those tires as I could stuff into the backseat and trunk of my car. I'd go to Oshkosh on Tuesdays, Shawano on Saturdays, and Seymour and De Pere on Sundays. I'd tell them, 'I'll make you guys a deal. You've got to come down and try it.' They would always say they didn't have money to buy the asphalt tires."

The deal was Grode would buy the runoffs (used asphalt tires) and give them to the dirt track drivers. It they didn't like running the tar, they'd simply give the runoff tires back. If they decided to stick with it, they'd reimburse Grode whatever amount he had paid for the runoffs. In short, the consignment-type tire deal with the dirt boys worked.

"I bought more damned tires than Richard Petty Enterprises," joked Grode. "They were $10 a piece used. I'd go to the Red, White and Blue races and buy the used ones from the bigger teams. I'd go to the guys who were running around here during the week and buy some from them at their shops, too, and take them to the dirt tracks. I never once got hung with a set of tires."

Grode got involved in the racing scene in 1971 when he built the motor for Cork Surprise.

"That was after I got out of the hospital that year," he said. "I had a car fall on me at the wrecking yard and I broke my back. (Grode was confined to a wheelchair after that.) After that, Dave Thompson and I built a Dodge Dart. We ran at Apple Creek and Shiocton. Dave was a Dodge guy like myself."

With Thompson as the driver, the team ran until 1974 at those tracks as well as Leo's Speedway in Oshkosh, and took occasional trips to the half-miles at Shawano Speedway and the Brown County Fairgrounds in De Pere. After the 1974 season, Grode sold his half of ownership in the car and took a new challenge – helping form the Fox River Racing Club.

"There already was the Wolf River Racing Club, which disbanded after the track in Shiocton closed in 1973," explained Grode. "So I just went along with Fox River Racing Club (name) after the Fox Valley Stock Car club basically ceased after Apple Creek closed. It just sort of stuck. It actually wasn't anything intentional."

KK Sports Arena did not host weekly racing prior to 1975.

"In some spots, there was grass growing through the track," said Grode. "It was just Red, White and Blue races there for a while."

The first year of the club's existence in 1975 featured Bob Seehawer as president, Ron Van Roy as vice president, Grode as secretary, and Ray Dietzen as treasurer. The track was still known as KK Sports Arena. The Thursday night program consisted of late models on the half-mile, a sportsman class on the inner quarter mile, which even included coupes driven by drivers like Bryce Spoehr, and many Apple Creek and Shiocton drivers who were stuck without a track. Figure 8s rounded out the weekly show.

"People thought we were crazy to try and resurrect a Thursday night racing program at WIR, because some other guys had gone belly up trying to do it," explained Grode. "Guys like Clyde Schumacher tried it when the half-mile was dirt. It didn't work. They didn't have a big turnout of cars. It was more than one guy could handle. Connie DeLeeuw tried and it went haywire. Then Joe (Van Daalwyk) got it back again.

"We had approached Joe about getting this going again. Because I was secretary in the winter of 1974, I'd negotiate a lot of stuff with Joe. He'd always say 'Spell it out! Spell it out!' He wasn't too bad to deal with if you knew what you were talking about. I'd go in his office, throw the figures and calculations on his desk and say, 'Here's what I think we can do.' "

Van Daalwyk took a puff of his cigar, scratched his head and told Grode, "Okay, let's do this."

Grode had recently graduated from the University of Wisconsin with a degree in marketing and advertising. While wheelchair-bound for the better part of his adult life, he refused to let that disability slow him down.

The club tried several different gimmicks to draw the fans to the races on Thursday nights.

"We started a scout night, where all scouts who were in their uniform were admitted free," said Grode. "I even had scout leaders from Milwaukee call me and come up. That was a successful promotion, along with the Big Wheel races we started. We started the Dash for Cash promotion. I'd go to the bank and get all these pennies, nickels, dimes and quarters. We'd go down the front straightaway and my future wife, Lois, would pour the coins out of the window of my '70 Dodge Charger. The announcer would count down from 3, 2, 1 and the kids would scramble for the coins. It was a hoot."

After consulting with K&K Insurance, the company that insured the weekly races at the track, Grode and company decided to give kids rides in race cars during the national anthem's pace lap. Shopping cart races were held at intermission with drivers and their pit crew members. Spectator eliminators were an added attraction on Thursday nights.

"We needed stuff like that to fill the show because honestly, some nights between all three classes, we'd be lucky to get thirty-five to forty cars," said Grode.

Things weren't always easy in the beginning for the club's leaders.

"I remember the second night we ran, financially we were in tough shape," said Grode. "We had spent what Joe (Van Daalwyk) had given us in startup money from the first week for expenses. So the second night of racing, I'm sitting in the office in the pit area and I only had $300 to pay the drivers in all three classes. That was it."

Van Daalwyk came around. He saw the long faces of the club officers and asked, "What's the problem?" Grode told him they were short to make the drivers payout. Van Daalwyk loaned them the $400 to make good on the payout the drivers had coming.

"Joe knew what we were trying to do and he was making money on concessions anyways, so he helped us out," said Grode. "Joe was good to work with as long as you knew what you were talking about. Obviously, we B.S.'ed him enough to convince him that we did indeed know what we were doing."

Not only was the effort ongoing to attract fans, it was to attract drivers as well.

"Ron Van Roy and I went to Adams-Friendship on one cold, winter night to one of their meetings to recruit the guys who ran Plover and the Wisconsin Rapids circuit," said Grode. "We weren't real well received at the time because they had Wausau, which ran on Thursday nights at the time. We told the drivers they were welcome to come. Some of the younger guys who were at that meeting came down to try racing by us. Butch Mierendorf (Waterloo) was there. It seemed as if the Trickles and the Detjens, Reffner and that had sort of a clique. The younger guys listened to us. Rich Somers started running by us. He was a Central Wisconsin guy. They knew we were there and what we were doing. I guess I can understand why we weren't that well received. It opened things up for the drivers who weren't so hot on the tar for them, middle-of-the-pack guys who could make some money by us. They couldn't make money racing against Trickle and Reffner and the like."

Several club members were pitching in – drivers, fans, car owners and

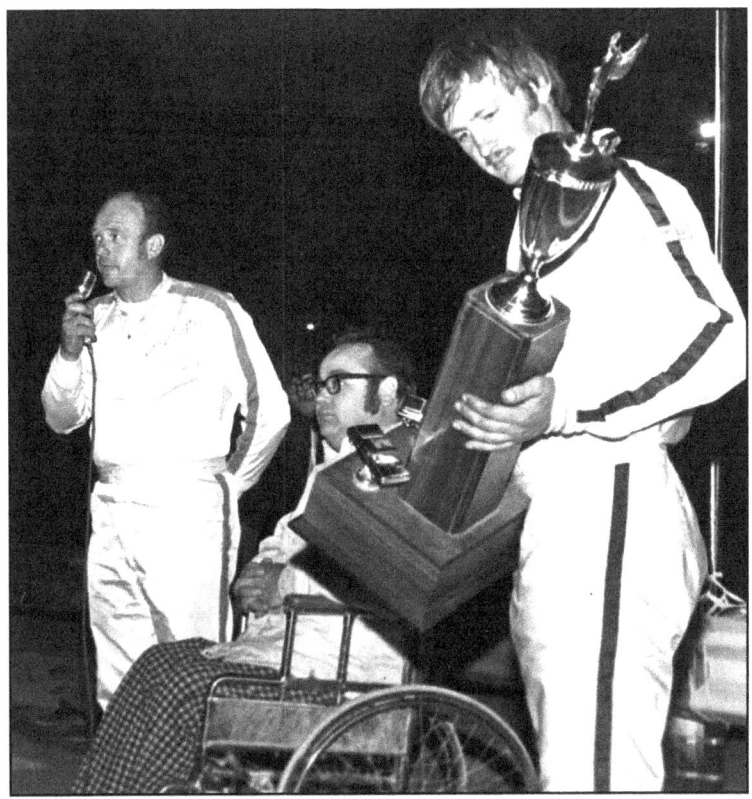
(From left) Jerry "Medina" Smith, Rene Grode and Larry Schuler at WIR in 1977 (Pete Vercauteren photo, Rene Grode collection)

club officers – to build the Thursday night show and get the word out in the various Fox Valley communities. Locals would donate items such as bottles of booze for fan giveaways. Van Daalwyk would give away tickets to the Red, White and Blue shows. Grode did ticket giveaway swaps with the local dirt tracks. It was all an attempt to build fan attendance at the relatively new Thursday night program.

Among the local drivers who supported the Thursday night races from the beginning in 1975 were Roger Regeth (Kimberly), Pete Parker (Kaukauna), and JJ Smith (Appleton), all of whom were some bigger names already on the local dirt track scene.

"What we found were some guys who weren't necessarily front runners on dirt, like Stan "The Man" Gracyalny, Roehborn and Mike Kelly, would come by us and run better and make more money. They were more like mid-pack guys by us on asphalt."

With the Thursday night program being so new to many drivers, there was quite a gap between the front running cars and the back markers – especially on the half-mile.

"That gap was so great that we had set up a rule where a driver had to turn in at least a 29-second lap in order to make the feature," Grode pointed out. "We didn't want anybody to get run over. We had five or six really fast cars – guys like Rich Somers and Larry Schuler for example, because they already had the experience on the tar."

With that great disparity in half-mile speeds, Grode came up with an idea.

"We decided to create the six-for-six fast dash. That way those fastest six cars each night, who were normally head and shoulders above the rest of the field anyways, could have their own race in lieu of a heat, and it was normally one helluva race."

Once word of the Thursday night program spread through word of mouth and the racing trade papers, drivers would come from all parts of the Midwest – even on a week night. One of them was Larry Schuler.

"(Schuler) would come up every week for a few seasons all the way from Lockport, Illinois," said Grode. "Schuler was a really nice guy. He was a lineman for the power company down there. His dad, Lee, would bring the car up, and Larry would usually pull up later, barely in time to time trial. Larry had little pieces of metal, it was like shaft. He would take those pieces of shaft, different length ones, and put them on different places on the car. And if it lined up, the car was good to go. If it wasn't, he'd start changing shocks and springs and stuff like that. Screw jacks, too. He had a system down and that car was fast, very fast."

"We were pulling in guys to run weekly by us from Wisconsin Rapids and the Wausau area. We even had some tow up from Indiana on occasion, too – on a Thursday night. After a while, Rich Somers came. Alan Kulwicki came eventually. Tony Strupp. Al Schill. Those Milwaukee guys came up. They were all great guys and they supported us well in the beginning."

From a public relations standpoint, De Pere native Gary Vercauteren, who lived in nearby Chilton, went to bat for the club in its early years.

"Gary was a great guy who wrote a lot of good press about the club," said Grode. "At first, I had a problem with Gary because I equated him with Joe and the race track, which was kind of against us a little bit in the beginning. But I later found out that was not true. The man loved racing. We got to be really good friends. I bought a '65 Barracuda from him one time. He got me into the *Chilton Times Journal* he was running. The whole family had been involved in racing for quite a few years and Gary really did a great job for us getting the word out."

By 1977, the FRRC had mustered up a $25,000 point fund that was split between the club drivers. Toward the end of that season, weekly crowds of nearly 4,000 people attended the races. Grode remained president of the club in 1978, but stepped down after that.

"I got married that year," he said. "I had to put more hours in at work at Valley Auto Parts. I was building a house. I needed to put more effort into my personal life. I was attending races five to six nights a week. It just got to be too much."

The FRRC remains one of the strongest, active club-run weekly racing programs in the Midwest.

"You forge relationships after thirty years," Grode said. "Guys who were your enemies back then now are your friends. You always had your chronic bitchers, and you've got the guys who just come to run and are happy you got the deal going. It was a great ride and a wonderful learning experience for me in those four years."

In recent years, Grode has been a driving force in management behind the successful Mackville Tractor Pulls. He still resides in Black Creek.

Figure 8 drivers avoid each other while passing through the 'X' in the middle of the track at WIR. (Bob Bergeron photo)

Figure 8
Meet in the Middle

They've been called a little "off" at times. Unwrapped, nuts, crazy, fearless and all of the above come up in a conversation about Figure 8 drivers.

Think about it for a minute. A race track where you turn both left and right, and weave your way through an "X" where the crowd cheers and actually encourages collisions? The radio ads that blared over the radio stations in Green Bay and the Fox Valley over the decades always included a tag at the end with "And don't forget the smack dab, meet-'em-in-the-middle, wild and crazy Figure 8s!"

The Figure 8 division is as much a part of Wisconsin International Raceway history as anything. It's been a part of the Fox River Racing Club since its inception. Most of the time, the Figure 8 drivers are the last to compete – whether it's a Thursday night show or when the Red White and Blue races were held on Sunday afternoons.

Figure 8 drivers were always the nightcap of the show, if you will. As a whole, they've always had to exercise patience and wait until late at night to do their thing. And most of the time the fans – no matter how late it was – would stick around to watch the mayhem at the "X."

Darboy's Terry Van Roy has won ten Figure 8 championships – more than anyone else in the track's history. What's more amazing about Van Roy's accomplishments is that he has managed to win those championships and race in the Figure 8s for four decades using only two cars.

"I've still got my first Figure 8 car," said Van Roy. "It was a '70 Monte Carlo. I remember the first year I ran was 1985. Back then, the only class on the quarter-mile was the sportsman. I couldn't afford to race any other division, so Figure 8 for me was the cheapest way into the sport."

To say Van Roy has gotten his money's worth out of his Figure 8 cars is an understatement.

"They get wrecked a lot, so I've had to put new front stubs and new tails on them at times over the years," said Van Roy. "There's no way you could run those cars that many years without fixing them up."

What makes a good Figure 8 racer?

"You've got to be a little crazy," admitted Van Roy. "The older you get, though, you do learn the patience and timing. You get used to the guys and know who you could go through the 'X.' You know Danny (Gracyalny) is gonna blast through the 'X' every time without stopping. You just don't know."

It was a tough road to hoe for Van Roy in his first few outings on the Figure 8 circuit.

"I actually got hit in the middle the first few times I drove Figure 8," said Van Roy. "It was during a Red White and Blue race. I didn't let it slow me down, though. The cars were real crude. You'd just go to a junkyard, build a roll cage, put it in and go racing."

Van Roy is a versatile racer who also competes in the super stock class on the quarter-mile, as well as area dirt tracks in a grand national. He's won several super stock titles as well.

"It's really a totally different game chasing a Figure 8 title," explained Van Roy. "You've always got to have some luck on your side. You are always bumping and banging guys, so the risk of cutting a tire is much more apparent."

***

It was a collision with a friend's former police squad car and a deer that launched Danny Gracyalny's Figure 8 racing career.

"When I was fifteen years old, my buddy Pat Braun had a '71 Buick Skylark that used to be a Waupaca County squad car," said Gracyalny. "Pat's dad had a tree farm in Waupaca. He hit a deer with that car one night coming home from that tree farm. It was a wreck, and Braunie and I decided to make that into a Figure 8 car. It was in 1981."

The two friends built the car while Gracyalny took over as the machine's hired gun. It didn't take the fearless Gracyalny long to establish his presence on the "X."

"Basically, I go full throttle through the 'X' and never stop," said Gracyalny, who's paid the price on more than one occasion for his daring antics. "I wrecked so many cars in the early years. It was so bad that every Friday morning after the races, my dad's neighbor, who was a farmer named Greg Van Handel, would come over with his Massey-Ferguson tractor. We'd use that to pull the engines out of the cars I'd wreck. It didn't matter if it was raining. He'd see the smashed car and we'd pull it out. We didn't have a cherry picker. We'd use a bucket on a tractor and a chain to pull those motors out. He'd be there rain or shine. It was almost a weekly thing because I had no fear."

That lack of fear led to one of the worst wrecks in track history in 2007. Gracyalny collided with veteran Kenny Van Wychen. The wreck was so loud it sounded like a shotgun blast had gone off in Gracyalny's ear.

"I had gotten up to almost 85 miles per hour because I had changed a flat tire and I got that speed up on the half-mile front stretch. When I got back and we collided, I got hit so hard I ended up tight against the inner guardrail to the backstretch on the half-mile."

The wreck broke Gracyalny's shoulder blade. One man's misfortunate turned into another man's opportunity.

With Gracyalny unable to race, his crew was bound and determined to get the car back together. Gracyalny's brother, Dave, and brother-in-law, Chris Larocque, helped rebuild the battered racer. Gracyalny's nephew, Craig VandeWettering, answered the call.

"I was hanging around Uncle Danny's shop and we fixed that car up," said VandeWettering, the 2015 and 2016 Figure 8 champion. "Danny was out with the injury. His car was a mess, and Danny said if I helped fix the car, I could drive it the following Thursday night. But the catch was I couldn't stop

Craig VandeWettering poses with his car following a Figure 8 victory. (www.danlewisphoto.net)

for the 'X' – I had to run through it."

VandeWettering took Uncle Danny up on his challenge.

"Everyone around Danny's shop was giving me a hard time all week, saying that I would probably chicken out and stop at the 'X,' " said VandeWettering. "I said, 'Absolutely not! You will see fireworks this week!' I'll never forget as I went out on the track and took the green flag, I was wobbling so bad down the straightaway my teeth were chattering. Apparently no one ever checked to see if the rear end in car was okay. An axle was bent so bad that it was ready to break."

The third-generation Kaukauna driver survived his inaugural run and went on to have a career filled with several wins and championships along the way.

"Driving Figure 8 is turning both ways, focusing on what is going on in front of you, and trying to find a way around a guy," explained VandeWettering. "Believe me, it's tough to pass on the outside on the Figure 8 track, but on top of all that it's still timing stuff out for the 'X.' You have to look across the track when you're going through one corner at the opposite corner, and judge at that point if you are gonna have enough to beat someone through to avoid an accident."

***

When it comes to colorful characters on the Figure 8 circuit, Kaukauna's own Kenny Van Wychen most certainly takes the cake. Van Wychen's been racing that division for more than forty-five years and is considered "The Dean" of the class. It's seldom you'll see a Figure 8 race without Van Wychen's number 52 racer spinning around the track. Van Wychen picked the number 52 because he was born in 1952.

"I tell these kids I race against that I've got more laps on this track going backward than they do going forward," joked Van Wychen, who is sixty-four years old.

Van Wychen grew up a mile down the road from the track and climbed behind the wheel of a Figure 8 car for the first time in 1971. It was his buddy, fellow Figure 8 racer Joe Jaeckels, who got him into racing.

"Joe's dad had a farm across the street from the race track," recalled Van Wychen. "We'd take cars down this lane into a woods and we'd smash them up. We'd roll them over. He had a tractor with a big chain. He'd pick them up, we'd fix them up and roll them over again."

Jaeckels had a wild idea that they should go race the Figure 8s across the street at WIR and get paid.

"To me, it was like a dream to get paid to wreck cars!" exclaimed Van Wychen, who was nineteen years old when he entered his first Figure 8 race. "I remember it was a Sunday when they ran the spring opener. I was hooked after that. My first car was a '63 Chevy."

Since that first race, Van Wychen said he can count on two hands how many Figure 8 races he's missed in forty-five years.

"I haven't missed many, I can tell you that," he said.

Van Wychen won the weekly Fox River Racing Club title in 1977, has won the Red White and Blue series, the Eve of Destruction, and even a mini-series thrown together with the Slinger Figure 8 drivers.

"The Eve of Destruction is sort of like the Super Bowl for us Figure 8 guys," said Van Wychen. "We race for a little more pay. And the biggest thing is we'll race in front of 12,000 people that night. I remember the first few years we did the Eve, the crowds seemed to double in size each year."

Over the years, Van Wychen has seen car counts in the division fluctuate.

"I remember the most cars we had one night was thirty-two," he said.

"Then we decided that night it was too many, so they made a rule to run no more than fifteen cars in a race. So for a while, we'd have two races a night."

With running Figure 8s for five decades, Van Wychen has had his share of bad collisions at the "X."

"Yeah, I usually go through at least one car a year," he said. "They hospitalized me one night after I got hit so bad my leg smashed up against the roll bar. We didn't have any padding back then. They kept me overnight in the hospital because I had broken blood vessels all up and down my leg."

Van Wychen's chief competitors over the years included Al Bangart, the Gracyalny brothers, Terry Van Roy and Rick Zieler.

"To be a good Figure 8 driver, you've got to pay attention to what's going on all the time. Every half a lap you've got that intersection, and like Dirty Harry says, 'You've got to ask yourself, do you feel lucky tonight?'"

As for the future, Van Wychen still has two Figure 8 cars at his disposal that are in what he calls "decent shape."

"I promised the wife that when these cars get used up that I'll be done, so who knows how long that will be," Van Wychen joked.

***

As a young fan in the stands, Appleton's Rick Kaufert acted like a kid on Christmas morning when the Figure 8 cars would roll onto the track for the final event of the evening.

"I used to chum around with Jeff Wolhrabe, and his dad, Lenny Wolhrabe, was like a father figure to me growing up," said Kaufert. "I used to watch those guys race at Apple Creek. I went to a lot of races with those guys on Thursday nights and I fell in love with the Figure 8s right away."

Kaufert, who was the 1993 Figure 8 champion, got his initiation into the class in 1984.

"There were a lot of cars, some nights over thirty," said Kaufert. "We'd have fifteen in each race and there were always two races. It was a real popular draw back then."

Like any Figure 8 driver who sticks with it for any number of years, Kaufert's had his share of wrecks at the "X."

"I clipped Lee Roy Heindel one night in the driver's door and neither one of us let off," said Kaufert. "I flipped end over end and barrel-rolled twice.

Lee Roy wound up in the hospital overnight with a punctured lung. It's just one of the hazards of racing Figure 8. It's exciting, but dangerous. I don't see too many late model guys who want to come out and give it a try. You've got to be fearless."

1985 Figure 8 Drivers

03	Al Derks	Combined Locks
05	Randy Krueger	Kaukauna
2	Jack Unmuth	Appleton
4	Mark Unmuth	Appleton
5	Mike Bunnell	Neenah
7	Doug Brown	Neenah
8	Lance Freeman	Menasha
14	Dan Manteufel	Appleton
15	John Bunnell	Neenah
22	Dan Ashauer	Kaukauna
25	Scott Belongea	Appleton
26	Terry Benner	Oshkosh
28	Randy Beattie	Little Chute
33	Ron Kowalke	Kimberly
41	Tom Spierowski	Neenah
43	Dan Buechler	Kaukauna
44	Dan Urbschat	Oshkosh
47	Steve Wittmann	Menasha
49	Dan Gracyalny	Kaukauna
52	Ken Van Wychen	Kaukauna
53	John Brewe	Darboy
54	Jesse VanLinn	Black Creek
56	Mark Van Veghel	Little Chute
57	Al Bangart	Kaukauna
62	Jeff Beschta	Appleton
81	Mike King	Appleton
83	Wayne Uttech	Neenah
88	Dave Uttech	Menasha
95	Ted Lamers	Kaukauna
96	Randy Rahn	Brillion
99	Mike St. Cyr	Menasha

Figure 8 Track Champions

2020 - Nick Osberg
2019 - Mike Meyerhofer
2018 - Craig Vanderwettering
2017 - Terry Van Roy
2016 - Craig Vandewettering
2015 - Craig Vandewettering
2014 - Craig Vandewettering
2013 - Jared Baughman
2012 - Craig Vandewettering
2011 - Dan Gracyalny
2010 - Dan Gracyalny
2009 - Terry Van Roy
2008 - Jeff Wohlrabe
2007 - Terry Van Roy
2006 - Donald Van Camp
2005 - Donald Van Camp
2004 - Terry Van Roy
2003 - Jeff Beschta
2002 - Terry Van Roy
2001 - Terry Van Roy
2000 - Terry Van Roy
1999 - Randy Theimer
1998 - Dan Gracyalny
1997 - Terry Van Roy
1996 - Dan Gracyalny
1995 - Terry Van Roy
1994 - Terry Van Roy
1993 - Rick Kaufert
1992 - Terry Van Roy
1991 - Dan Gracyalny
1990 - Dan Gracyalny
1989 - Terry Van Roy
1988 - Dan Gracyalny
1987 - Dan Gracyalny
1986 - Jeff Beschta
1985 - Dan Gracyalny
1984 - Randy Rahn
1983 - Randy Rahn
1982 - Dave Uttech
1981 - Randy Rahn
1980 - Tom Munes
1979 - Tom Munes
1978 - Rick Zieler
1977 - Kenny Van Wychen

Family patriarch Stan "The Man" Gracyalny in 1974. (Pete Vercauteren photo)

The Gracyalny Family
Born to Race

Stan "The Man" Gracyalny simply loved racing.

Originally from Kimberly, the auto body man raced for more than sixty years, most of that time at KK Sports Arena later known as Wisconsin International Raceway. In fact, Gracyalny's last time behind the wheel – of any type of motorized vehicle – was in 2004 when he was eighty years old in the super stock division. When Gracyalny hit the wall, his kids, who also launched their own racing careers, knew something was wrong.

"When we took Dad to the doctor the next day, they found out he had a blood clot during the race," said Dave Gracyalny. "They figured it actually blinded him and he couldn't see for a bit during the race. That was the last time he ever drove anything."

It didn't bother Stan if he won many races or not.

"He simply loved to race," said Gracyalny's widow, Sharon, who first met Stan when he was racing at Apple Creek in 1961. "I never would have taken that away from him."

Of the four kids Stan and Sharon had together, Dave is the oldest at fifty-four as of this writing. Dave competed in super stock, Figure 8 and even dabbled on the dirt for a time. Daughter Leeann (Laroque) is fifty-three, and although she never raced, married a super stock racer in Chris Laroque.

Danny Gracyalny is fifty-two and has raced virtually anything with four tires and a motor. Daughter Jessie (Gracyalny) Van Roy made history at WIR by becoming the first woman to win a race there in the super stock division in 1997.

The Gracyalny kids were born into the sport. The family grew up near Kaukauna where Stan ran his own shop, Stan's Auto Body. It didn't take long for Danny Gracyalny to learn how to paint.

"Stan would come in from the shop and say, 'I can't get anything done. I'm always tripping over Danny,'" said Sharon Gracyalny. "On race nights, I was never able to take part in the Powder Puff races for the wives. I was busy with those little kids in the stands!"

"I remember standing on a five-gallon paint thinner can painting cars when I was nine years old," said Danny Gracyalny. "Years later, I bought a 1970 Firebird for thirty-five dollars. I restored it for a shop class in high

(Left to right) Hank Calmes, Stan Gracyalny, Joe Jaeckels, Russ Keberlein, trophy queen Debbie Ashauer, Dick Trickle, and Danny Gracyalny in 1988. (Pete Vercauteren photo)

school and the teachers didn't think I even did it. They thought somebody older did it."

As Dave and Danny grew into their teenage years, they would accompany their dad on many a racing trip.

"I remember we were racing somewhere one night and Dad had a Ford truck with the ramps on the back," recalled Danny Gracyalny. "In the heat race, he lost the battery. It flew out of the car somewhere on the track and they never found it. He took the battery out of the hauler and used that to race the next race. He lost that battery, too. So here we are at the races one night with no battery. He somehow conned some other driver into borrowing us a battery to use. We made it home that night on a hope and a prayer, turning the motor off when we'd coast down the hills. It was crazy."

Danny began racing Figure 8s when was old enough to get his driver's license. Dave was the late bloomer of the three kids.

"I didn't race until I was twenty-five," said Dave Gracyalny. "I was doing burnouts and that on the streets and I wrecked a transmission, and Dad told me, 'You should really go racing,' and so I ran Figure 8 in Al Bangart's car. He had it set up where you sat in the middle of the car. He went to Arizona for two weeks, so I raced his car. It was in the middle of the car. You had to let go of the steering wheel when you went to turn right."

"I remember one of the first times I went out, I got my car totaled out in the X," said Dave continued. "But I still won the race."

Dave Gracyalny would eventually hang up his helmet. He served as a corner worker and flagman for several area tracks, including WIR.

When it came to Danny Gracyalny starting his racing career, he pulled a little white lie.

"Danny actually lied about his age. He had to be sixteen to race," admitted Dave Gracyalny. "He was only fifteen."

It didn't take long for Danny Gracyalny to race anything and everything he could get his hands on. It did not matter if it was dirt or asphalt. If it had a motor and four tires, it was fair game. In 1993, he drove a super late model car at WIR with a paint scheme identical to Jeff Gordon's number 24.

"We even had sponsorship from DuPont," said Danny Gracyalny, who beat future NASCAR star Matt Kenseth at the line one night to win the feature. Danny has the distinction of being the only driver in Fox River

Racing Club history to compete in five divisions on the same night – late model, sportsman, super stock, sport truck and Figure 8.

Danny filled in for Mike Butz's super late model in the late 1990s when Terry Baldry was injured. Butz was quoted then as stating, "Danny Gracyalny has as much raw talent as Matt Kenseth."

Jessie Gracyalny came along a few years later, and she and her dad became the first father-daughter team to run at WIR in the super stock class. "Dad never pushed me into it," explained Jessie.

During her first year racing, Jessie tangled with Randy Van Roy.

"I sent Randy rocking into the pickers," said Jessie. "Randy thought I was blocking for Chris Laroque and he gave me the one-finger salute while we were under caution, and I thought to myself, 'That sonofabitch!'"

There was a mini feud of sorts between the Gracyalnys and the Van Roys. The grudge centered on Danny Gracyalny and Terry Van Roy in the Figure 8 class. One night, Ron Van Roy, Terry's dad, went after Danny while Danny was still belted into his car.

"He tried pulling me out of the car," said Danny Gracyalny. "They wanted to suspend Ron, but I talked to (FRRC club officers) and told them not to. I was in a points battle with Terry (Van Roy), and I didn't want to win a championship that way. I wanted to earn it on the track."

Little did Jessie Gracyalny know, she would later end up dating Randy Van Roy and eventually marrying him and becoming Jessie Van Roy.

"Ron Kohl (fellow racer) had a little bit to do with us getting together," said Jessie. "He saw me out one night away from the track with my hair down, with makeup on and out of my racing suit. He said, 'Is that Jessie Gracyalny?' and things just sort of progressed from there."

"Jessie came to Stan and I and asked, 'What would you think if I married Randy Van Roy?'" said Sharon Gracyalny. "After they got married, Ron (Van Roy) and everybody else backed off from the feud. So that's pretty much done with."

"It's actually a good thing she married Randy, because that way she could continue racing since he's from a racing family," said Danny Gracyalny. "Heck, a couple of years ago I raced one night at Luxemburg, and who was on my pit crew? Terry Van Roy. So yeah, the rivalry has sort of fizzled out really."

Stan "The Man" Gracyalny was able to attend races for several years as a spectator. He passed away December 22, 2013, at the age of ninety. Each summer, a "Stan the Man" race is held on the quarter-mile in his honor. Even when the rain isn't there on "Stan the Man" night, rainbows have been known to pop up in the sky over WIR.

"We know he's there in spirit," said Jessie.

Jessie (Gracyalny) Van Roy in 2011.
(Chuck Look photo, Jessie Van Roy collection)

Jim Sauter poses with a Gene Wheeler car in the early 1980s. (Pete Vercauteren photo)

Gene Wheeler
Cubic Dollars

Gene Wheeler estimates he's spent literally millions over the years on race cars during his racing career as both a driver and car owner at Wisconsin International Raceway. Much of that was spent writing checks on late models that toured the half-mile in the 1980s through 2009. The Appleton car owner always seemed to have the latest trick chassis, the best bolt on parts, and the sharpest-looking cars that money could buy.

As a result, Wheeler's top-notch rides were attractive to a number of hired guns over the years. When big-name NASCAR drivers rolled into town for big specials such as the Dixieland 250, ARTGO promoter John McKarns often called upon Wheeler to field rides for the likes of Darrell Waltrip, Neil Bonnett, Ernie Ervin, Kyle Petty, Dave Marcis and Buddy Baker.

"(The promoters) would usually give me tires and free pit passes for doing it, and we'd have a crash clause written up," explained Wheeler. "We never had to use them, though. Bonnett was a real nice guy. Ervin really raced the car hard. He was out to win."

A number of local weekly racers wheeled Wheeler's race cars over the years as well. They included his own son, Rod Wheeler, Bucky Wagner,

JJ Smith, Roger Regeth, Dave Valentyne, Dave Watson, "Smilin' Clyde" Schumacher, Axel Dahlberg, Lyle Nabbefeldt, Al Stepan, Glen Bessette, and Jim Courtney.

"I was fourteen years old, and a friend named Jack Nystrom from Appleton and I got a car from Sam Malosky's Motor Sales in the Valley," Wheeler said. "Sam had a '44 two-door sedan he donated to me and my buddy, and we built a race car out of it. We got a flathead Ford motor from him and we went racing with it. That's how it got started."

Wheeler and Nystrom got their start running Outagamie Speedway in Appleton.

"We'd run Shiocton for many years, too," said Wheeler. "KK Sports Arena (later WIR) wasn't even open at the time."

Wheeler fielded cars that would race both on the dirt and the asphalt in the roaring '70s, with Regeth and JJ Smith at the helm. Smith's famous "Tweety Bird" car sparkled and was a showstopper wherever it went. With Smith driving Wheeler's Boyce Trackburner built in Chicago, the pair nabbed dozens of dirt track feature wins and were perennial front runners Thursday nights on the tar.

In 1980, dirt track racing was dying in Northeast Wisconsin. Tracks in De Pere and Seymour were closed, in part because of the feud between rival promoters Jack Peters and Paul Kaczrowski, who were battling against each other on Sunday nights. As a result, many race teams began converting their late models to compete on Thursday nights on WIR's pavement full time.

"In '79 I had built a brand new Holman Moody USAC car for Jim (Sauter) and he became a hired gun for us," Wheeler said. "He stuck with us on Thursday nights pretty much after that."

Two former NASCAR stars were a pair of ringers who drove for Wheeler over the years: Sauter and Marcis.

"Those two were real good friends who both cut their teeth starting in the Central Wisconsin racing circuit in the mid-1960s," said Wheeler, adding both men were masters at chassis and setup. "Those guys both were sharp, real sharp."

It wasn't until Sauter, who would later become a regular on NASCAR's Winston Cup circuit, drove for Wheeler that he collected his first track championship as a car owner.

"I believe we won all but one race that year (1981) and the title," said Wheeler. "That was a dominant race car that year, no doubt."

The Necedah driver followed up that dominating performance by winning the ARTGO Challenge Series title in 1982.

Sauter wasn't afraid to take a chance. That got him into hot water on more than one occasion. One night in June 1981, during the "six-for-six" fast dash, Sauter tapped Oneida's Wayne Roffers and spun him. Roffers, a big-hearted driver who also possessed a short fuse, stormed over with a sledgehammer and stated, "If I can't run the feature, you ain't either," and started hammering on the windshield of Wheeler's car. The team made the repairs and made it out for the feature with a new windshield installed.

"Jim wouldn't take a back seat to no one," exclaimed Wheeler. "I mean, he won the ARCA 300 race that one year at Daytona. He spun the guy out on the last lap to win."

When it was all said and done, Sauter was Wheeler's hired gun for nineteen seasons, the same number of years that Smith drove for Wheeler.

"Sauter was probably the best driver who ever sat in my car," said Wheeler. "He just knew the car inside and out. He could change a car over at the track like nobody else. Not even close. He'd go underneath the car and wasn't afraid to get right in there."

Wheeler always fielded a car with the potential to win every week, often with the most up-to-date, latest-and-greatest of technology that was around at that time.

"We didn't always win too many championships, but were always a threat to win," said Wheeler. "Jim (Sauter) won a title with us at Kaukauna and ARTGO. Rod (Wheeler) won a title on the quarter-mile in the sportsman class and one on the half-mile."

Wheeler pointed out the team only ran for the Thursday night title one year with Sauter, and that was in 1981.

"We were traveling with ARTGO a lot the following season and we actually missed a few Thursday nights because of it," he said.

Sauter was one tough customer. Despite battling cancer and a broken foot suffered in a WIR wreck, it did not slow him down.

"Jim broke his foot in a wreck one Thursday night," Rod Wheeler recalled. "The following week we made a brace for him. We had to sit Jim in the race car to fit the brace for him. He raced even when he wasn't feeling well. He was tough, real tough."

Sauter basically raced for a living while with Wheeler.

"Our arrangement with Jim was a 60/40 split with the prize money, with Jim taking 40 percent of the winnings," said Gene Wheeler. "We've won with him at places like Rockford and Grundy Speedways (both in Illinois). We even ran some ASA races with Jim that were somewhat close from a schedule standpoint, like Minnesota State Fair, Milwaukee Mile and at Nashville, too. He was one of the best."

Sauter passed away on October 31, 2014, after a brief illness at the age of 71.

"JJ (Smith) was just very conscious and he wasn't overly aggressive," said Gene Wheeler. "He was patient. He'd sort of take his time and let things happen. He did a real good job for me and won a lot of races."

But Wheeler had another driver from Western Wisconsin who, as far as the dirt tracks went, was the best.

"That was Leon Plank, by far," said Wheeler. "That guy, when I still fielded dirt cars, could win anywhere we ever went. There would be a hole and Plank would be in there. He didn't care if the fenders got tore off."

Another controversial driver Wheeler had in the early '70s was "The Bear," Roger Regeth.

"To me, first place is the only place – second place is the first loser. Roger was the same way," said Wheeler. "He didn't care how he got there. He was very aggressive."

While Wheeler spent tons of his own money through his long time business, Appleton Auto Wrecking (now called Appleton Auto Recyclers) he also was able to secure some decent sponsors along the way.

"We had Old Style beer when Rod ran, and before that we had Boyce Trackburner Chassis out of Chicago," said Wheeler. "When Sauter ran for me, we got free motors from Baker Racing Engines. We worked hard for a lot of years to get to the point where we'd get that sponsorship."

Having been retired from racing for quite some time now, Wheeler spends his time at his Special Memories Zoo in Greenville. The zoo features several exotic animals and is open from May through September.

"I've got no regrets," he said. "It's been a great ride."

Rod Wheeler after another victory at WIR in 2006. (www.danlewisphoto.net)

Rod Wheeler
The Villain

"Hot Rod" Wheeler was a combination of the cartoon character Richie Rich and the villain, Black Bart.

The Appleton Ace was a polarizing figure on the Thursday night racing scene at Wisconsin International Raceway from the 1980s until he decided to hang up his helmet in 2009. There was no quarter asked, and none given when Wheeler strapped into his racer. Wheeler won an estimated sixty feature wins in the sportsman and late model classes. He captured the Fox River Racing Club late model crown in 2005 and was a Red, White and Blue state champion in 1998.

Wheeler had the privilege of driving in the best equipment possible over the years, provided by his dad, Gene Wheeler. He had the best stuff money could buy, and "Hot Rod" had the talent to match. Wheeler was a true "checkers or wreckers" kind of driver, always going for the win or being willing to destroy the car in the process of chasing that checkered flag.

With a start on the dirt tracks at the age of sixteen, Wheeler won his first dirt track race he ever entered. It was at the Brown County Fairgrounds in De Pere in 1978.

"I remember I was driving JJ's (Smith) backup car. I thought I was going really fast, but afterwards I realized I wasn't going very fast at all," laughed Wheeler. "The car was number 36. It was an Ed Sanger chassis."

Wheeler worked the half-mile dirt tracks at De Pere in 1978 and 1979, and at Shawano from 1978 to 1980.

"I really learned about car control running on the dirt, and I think it made me a better driver on the asphalt," said Wheeler. "A guy that runs well on the dirt can run the asphalt pretty easily. You don't panic at all when the car breaks loose on asphalt. So in my opinion, the dirt tracks are the way to start a racing career."

After De Pere closed following the 1979 season, Wheeler ran both the dirt at Shawano on Saturday nights and the half-mile in the late model class at WIR.

"The cars really weren't that specialized back then," recalled Wheeler. "To run Thursdays, we'd put the glass windshield in, bolt some asphalt tires on and go racing. For Saturdays, we'd pop the windshield out, put a screen in, dirt track tires, and that was pretty much it."

After the 1980 season, Wheeler took a couple of years off from behind the wheel to serve as a key crew member for Jim Sauter's dominating run racing Gene Wheeler's cars in 1981 and 1982.

"I learned a lot from JJ (Smith) being on their crew, but I probably learned the most from Sauter," said Rod Wheeler. "I didn't race and just helped Jim for those two years. He was just phenomenal at chassis setup. They all say (Dick) Trickle was great. Sauter, in my opinion was just as good. I mean we'd go all over the country and win. We could take Jim and figured we had a chance to win anywhere we went. And I mean anywhere."

1980 was the year the Thursday night program at WIR exploded in popularity. The large grandstand swelled each night with thousands of screaming fans. The pit area was filled to capacity with drivers from as far north as Michigan's Upper Peninsula and as far south as the Chicagoland suburbs and dozens of towns and cities in between.

"The dirt tracks were starting to die," said Wheeler. "Like everything, racing goes in cycles. The 9:1 compression motor rule at that time had a lot to do with the success at WIR. Dirt rules were getting a bit out of hand. Guys could build a car and an affordable motor and go racing on asphalt."

A $4,000 claim rule on the entire motor was in effect. In Fox River Racing Club racing, no motor claim ever took place in the early years.

"We had carbs claimed and that," said Rod Wheeler, "but that was pretty much about it."

Needing more experience in driving through traffic, Wheeler bumped down to the quarter-mile to run the rough-and-tumble sportsman class when he climbed back behind the wheel in the mid- to late 1980s. The class was tough then – real tough.

"We'd have forty guys a night back then and there was a ton of talent in the old sportsman division," recalled Wheeler. "They had Jim Duchow, Pete Berken, Steve Smits, and Gary Stankevitz ran it. There was probably as much talent in that class on the quarter-mile as there was on the half-mile."

They would start fourteen cars in the sportsman feature, with a full invert. That meant the fastest qualifier always started dead last. FRRC officials awarded bonus points for top qualifiers in an effort to eliminate "sandbagging." Sandbagging was a practice in which some drivers would intentionally "dog it," or qualify with a slower time trial lap in an effort to land a spot closer to the front of the starting field.

One of the more popular asphalt late model chassis over the years was Wayne Lensing's Lefthander Chassis out of Northern Illinois.

"I'm pretty sure we were one of the first drivers up this way to have a Lefthander, and that was when Wayne was building them in his garage," said Wheeler.

Wheeler made the jump full time to the late model class on the half-mile in 1991. The team acquired sponsorship from Old Style beer. One of the toughest drivers Wheeler went toe-to-toe with on Thursday nights was eventual NASCAR Winston Cup champion Matt "The Brat" Kenseth. Kenseth was nicknamed "The Brat" because he was still a teenager when he was winning late model features across the Midwest.

"Matt was always tough, so was Jim Weber," Wheeler said. "Matt raced a lot and worked for Lefthander chassis at the time. That seat time he got running three or four nights a week helped him. Weber raced a lot, too, on the

ARTGO series and all the specials in Wisconsin."

Wheeler has the distinction of being involved in one of the worst wrecks in Thursday night history. During a late model feature in the late 1990s, he tangled with Pete Berken coming out of turn two.

"I was on the outside of Berken and we collided on the backstretch, and I literally flew out of the ballpark over the backstretch wall," recalled Wheeler. "I took out the big billboard and landed on the drag strip. I ended up flipping in the process."

Wheeler's spotter at the time, Donny Schwartz, was screaming on the radio to Rod immediately after the wreck.

"He yelled, 'Rod, talk to me! Rod talk to me!' I couldn't say anything because the radio flew right out of the car," Wheeler explained. "The car was totally junk, except the seat. I kept that and still have it to this day."

Suffering nothing more than a concussion, Wheeler, who was involved in a tight point championship battle at that time, was not to be denied.

"Dad bought Dickie Anderson's Howe chassis house car from Florida the following week," he said. Thus, Wheeler never missed a night of racing that year.

Wheeler's reputation was that of an aggressive driver. He was never afraid to take a chance. If he saw a hole on the track, he'd take it. Sometimes it worked. Sometimes there were crinkled fenders and quarter panels. As a result, the partisan crowds at WIR on Thursdays would either cheer or jeer "Hot Rod" loudly.

"One day during driver intros during a Red, White and Blue race, I was walking to my car after they announced my name," he said. "They were booing pretty good. Joel Laufer (fellow racer from Hartford) looks at my wife and says, 'Well, at least you know they're watching him. He's got to have the most fans.' So the booing never really did bother me."

Wheeler filled the role of villain and enjoyed it.

"You've got to have somebody there to fill the void. I wasn't there to make friends. Race cars are made for racing. We're here to put on a show. I was there to win. If you want to just go ride around, go to Highway 41. I really didn't care. I didn't have many friends. I pitted next to Mark Schroeder for years, so I mean I talked to him and all. But that was about it. I even got into it with him a couple of times. I never really did have many friends there.

"My Dad always taught me to be aggressive. That's how I drove. I told people, 'The beauty show is done after the first race. Let's get it on. The car shows are done.' These days, it seems everybody wants to be buddies with everyone else. They want to go to the bar and drink with them afterwards. I wasn't big on socializing with anybody. I always minded my own business."

Wheeler chased the ARTGO Challenge Series for a couple of seasons and raced the ASA Midwest Tour in 2007. His last full time season was in 2009.

"I had a tumor in my lung, and they said it was stage 4 lung cancer initially," said Wheeler. "They took a lobe out of my lung and they said it wasn't cancer. So I hung it up after that."

With his daughter involved heavily in high school softball, it helped make the decision easy to hang up the helmet. "That stuff seemed more important than racing every Thursday night."

Wheeler still gets his racing fix during the summer months. His stepson, Brock Saunders, has raced on the local dirt tracks with an IMCA northern sportmod.

"Brock go kart-raced for a while before that and we decided to make the jump," said Wheeler. "As far as I'm concerned, right now it's cheaper to run the dirt than the asphalt these days. You don't have to bolt on new tires every week on dirt. And if you wreck on dirt, you're not spending a whole ton of money fixing stuff. You wreck on the half mile at WIR and it's a front stub or a new tail section. Those expenses add up in a hurry."

Sponsorship is also tougher to get these days – especially on the asphalt.

"They don't even have a Budweiser or a Miller car running anymore on Thursday nights," said Wheeler. "The big sponsors just are not there to run WIR. That goes with the dirt, too. You get friends who'll give you $500 or $1,000 maybe. It's just more cost effective for us to run dirt. And he enjoys it."

In addition to his half-mile accomplishments, Wheeler won a sportsman championship on the quarter-mile in the mid-1980s. He also became the first driver in club history to win titles on both sized tracks. Since then, Appleton's Jeff Van Oudenhoven has also accomplished that feat.

"I was also the first driver to record a 14-second lap on the quarter-mile," Wheeler pointed out.

But of all "Hot Rod's" accomplishments, the one he is most proud of is his first 100-lap feature win in the mid-1990s.

"My mom was there that night, and that was the biggest accomplishment in my life next to my kids being born," said Wheeler, who was also the first local driver to win the Red, White and Blue. "No local before that had ever won a 100-lap special. Matt (Kenseth), Joe Shear, Steve Carlson, Jim (Sauter) was in that show running one of our other cars. I remember I passed Joe Shear with twenty laps to go. It was huge. All the big guns were there. Dick Trickle may have even been in that race. It was the Blue race in the mid-1990s. I backed that up with the Fall Invitational win they used to have."

Wheeler currently serves as crew chief on his stepson Brock's sportmod ride.

Roger Regeth (right) with Joe Verdegan and the WIR pace car during a 2016 visit. (Joe Verdegan photo)

Roger Regeth
The Bear

Roger "The Bear" Regeth may have more laps on Wisconsin International Raceway's half-mile than any other driver.

That's mainly because when he retired (and "unretired years later), Regeth picked up another gig that kept him on top of the local racing scene – driving the pace car on Thursday nights and for specials. Regeth's long-time sponsor, Les Stumpf Ford, has almost always supplied the pace car for WIR over the years.

First time at WIR. USAC stock car 1968. First-ever race. Regeth finished fourth in the track's first-ever paved race.

"I remember Ernie Derr came up from Iowa and won that day," recalled Regeth. "When (Dick) Trickle started coming over, it was always a case of who was going to get second because Dick won everything. I would always wind up leading, but after ten or fifteen laps, my tires would go away. We had faster tires, but they would go away real fast."

Although he is best known for his dominance on local dirt tracks in the 1970s, "The Bear" fared quite well for many seasons on Thursday nights at WIR in Fox River Racing Club action.

"I know I finished second in the points in late models at least three or four times over the years," recalled Regeth. "And when I ran on the quarter mile years later in the sportsman class, I won seven out of seven features one year with that Grand National."

Regeth was always a "hired gun," where he would drive someone else's equipment. Sometimes it was even just a one race deal.

Roger Regeth in 1978. (Pete Vercauteren photo)

"I remember one year John Burbridge came up from Milwaukee. He had a big block Camaro. He wasn't racing that day," Regeth said. "He had Jack Brewer out of Milwaukee as a driver, but instead he decided to put me in the car one night. We got up to third before a bracket on the rear end broke. We were fast, though."

The Les Stumpf Ford car Regeth drove for car owner Jerry Sheriff was a Camaro, which became quite a conversation piece in the state racing ranks as a Ford-sponsored Chevrolet.

"But that car was fast," said Regeth. "I bet you we won ten or twelve features with that car. Some customers came in and joked about it. Rumors ran rampant that we had ten motors stockpiled in the garage that Les Stumpf Ford bought us and such. That wasn't true."

What makes Regeth's accomplishments so impressive was the brutal schedule the crew was put through while also racing all the area dirt tracks.

"We'd race at Shawano on Saturday nights," said Regeth. "The crew would go home, take out the screen, replace the windshield, lower the car and take the rear end out of the car for the Red, White and Blue races here," said Regeth. "The crew would work all night. Then after WIR, we'd run Sunday nights at De Pere. Tuesday nights, we'd run on the dirt at Leo's Speedway in Oshkosh. For a while, Friday nights is when Seymour was running, so we'd run there, too."

Regeth had a solid pit crew, and he never turned a wrench on the car – ever.

"I'd walk out of the car, tell them what it was doing, and Mike (Randerson) and the crew would go to town on that car," said Regeth. "There was nobody better around at that time who could prepare a car than Mike Randerson. Nowadays you've got Toby Nuttleman (crew chief for Roush Fenway Developmental Driver Ty Majeski of Seymour), but nobody even came close to Mike Randerson back then. Not even close. He was the best. He could have gone down south and worked for any NASCAR team. He worked close with (Alan) Kulwicki and he worked with (former ASA crew chief) Howie Lettow. But Mike is such a family man. He's a great man."

As an employee for Les Stumpf Ford, Regeth often was still in Chicago at 3 p.m. on Thursday afternoons.

"So by the time I got to the track, we never really had a lot of time for any practice," explained Regeth. "We won our share of features and got quite a few second-place finishes in not only the points, but in the features, too."

Regeth dabbled with a Grand National sportsman car Friday nights at Chilton and in the Mid-American series. In 1992, Regeth won seventeen of twenty features that year on the dirt at Chilton.

"I think racing on dirt all those years really did make me a better asphalt driver," said Regeth. "And that's because when you'd have a push on the dirt, you could move and drive out of it. Jim Weber from Minnesota was one guy who could move that car around and actually drive a push out of the car. That's one thing I learned."

After Regeth hung up his helmet, he began driving the pace car.

"I did it in the late '70s, and after that I took over," said Regeth. "I've been doing it pretty much since. I missed one night in 2015 and one night in 2016. I'm 77 years old now and I can say I get to lead every feature!"

The Dixieland races provided opportunities for local drivers such as Oneida's Wayne Roffers to mix it up with the ARTGO tour's traveling stars. (Pete Vercauteren photo)

Dixieland
Traditional Tuesday Biggie

In 1981, ARTGO promoter John McKarns teamed up with Joe and Roger Van Daalwyk in seeking a big event for Wisconsin International Raceway – one that would draw top Winston Cup drivers.

"With those guys booked up most weekends, the date we sought was a Tuesday and that's how the Dixieland race got started," said Van Daalwyk. "The first Dixieland race we ran was an off weekend for the Cup guys in 1981, but after that we always ran that show the first Tuesday in August."

That first show in 1981 featured a twin 50-lap feature format with Larry Schuler and Jim Sauter each winning the mains, and Mark Martin was declared the overall winner. Over the years, many big-name Cup stars would show up to compete in the event, including Darrell Waltrip, Dale Earnhardt and Neil Bonnett.

"We'd usually put those guys in local car owners' backup cars like Gene Wheeler and such," said Van Daalwyk. "The event grew over the years."

The Tuesday tradition was established and the event soon became the "richest one day asphalt race in Wisconsin." The program was slightly tweaked over the years, with drivers from the NASCAR's southern All American Series competing. The event included live pit stops.

1997 was the last "true" ARTGO Dixieland 250 run under ARTGO rules. In 1998, it was promoted by ARTGO promotions, sanctioned by the now-defunct ReMax Challenge Series, and renamed "The Oneida Bingo and Casino 250." GameDay Sports Marketing promoted the Oneida-sponsored Tuesday race from 1999 through 2004.

In 2005, Gary Vercauteren leased the track for a "Tuesday night shootout" for the former ASA National Tour cars, with Stephen Leicht winning. There was no Tuesday race in 2006 due to the National Fireworks Convention and road construction.

The ASA Midwest Tour resurrected the event in 2007, with NASCAR ace Kyle Busch the winner while driving for Ashwaubenon native Richie Wauters. There was no event for a couple of years before John McKarns's son, Gregg, purchased the ASA Midwest Tour and resurrected the event under the ARCA Midwest Tour banner in 2015.

The largest car count in the event's history was seventy-four late models in 1987. The largest drivers' purse was in 1999, with $86,575 doled out among the feature field. The largest crowd was also in 1987, when 11,779 fans attended the "Traditional Tuesday Biggie."

NASCAR star Neil Bonnett (right) poses with his crew and a car supplied by Gene Wheeler for the 1981 Dixieland race at WIR. (Pete Vercauteren photo)

ARTGO Dixieland Winners at WIR

1981 – Mark Martin
1982 – Jim Sauter
1983 – Dick Trickle
1984 – Mark Martin
1985 – Butch Miller
1986 – Butch Miller
1987 – Dick Trickle
1988 – Butch Miller
1989 – Rich Bickle
1990 – Dick Trickle
1991 – Dick Trickle
1992 – Steve Holzhausen
1993 – Scott Hansen
1994 – Joe Shear
1995 – Bryan Reffner
1996 – Joe Shear
1997 – Steve Carlson
1998 – Steve Carlson
1999 – Scott Hansen
2000 – Brian Hoppe
2001 – Steve Carlson
2002 – Brian Hoppe
2003 – Steve Carlson
2004 – Steve Carlson
2005 – Stephen Leicht
2006 – No Race Held
2007 – Kyle Busch
2008 – Steve Carlson
2009 – Steve Carlson
2010 – Johnny Sauter
2011 – Tim Schendel
2012 – No Race Held
2013 – No Race Held
2014 – No Race Held
2015 – Nick Murgic
2016 – Dennis Prunty

Larry Detjens and his crew in 1981 at the Milwaukee Mile. (Pete Vercauteren photo)

Echoes of a Fatal Crash
How, and Why, Racing Lost Larry Detjens

(Reprinted from the *Green Bay Press-Gazette,* August 23, 1981)

"A lot of racing people have a fatalistic attitude, like if it's your time, it's your time. I don't believe in that. But you see something like this and I'll tell you, you start to wonder."

-Racing official John McKarns

By Tom Wheatley

They paid their respects to Larry Detjens last Sunday at the Wisconsin International Raceway.

Detjens, a 37-year-old stock car driver from Wausau, was killed in a freak accident Aug. 1 at the Kaukauna track.

Detjens was to have run in a special anniversary race last Sunday. It was to have been a day of celebration.

Instead, the pre-race ceremony was a solemn tribute. There was a gap in the parade where Detjens' No. 25 racer would have appeared. A black flag snapped in the pace car.

The crowd stood quietly, many of the fans wiping away tears. Then a youngster broke the heavy silence.

"What happened to Larry Detjens' car?" he asked.

What happened to Larry Detjens car?

Since the fatal accident three weeks ago, the people close to Detjens have been haunted by that question.

Nearly all agree the accident was a fluke.

"There were about 10 little things that came together," said John McKarns, president of ARTGO racing, who witnessed the crash. "If any one of those things had just a whisker different, Larry'd still be racing."

But during its emotional mourning for the popular Detjens, the racing community never really had time to establish the what and the why of his crash.

Rumors passed by word of mouth. Conflicting eyewitness accounts spread. Misinformation was printed.

"People all keep twisting this thing around," said driver Alan Kulwicki of Milwaukee, who was involved in the crash. Kulwicki has heard the rumors – that other drivers blamed him for the crash, that fights broke out in the pits, that he was forced to leave the track under police escort.

"That's not true," he said. "Not one of the other drivers ever said anything to me."

Even the cause of Detjens' death – impact with a guardrail – is widely misunderstood. "A lot of people still think the end of the guardrail came into the car," said McKarns of ARTGO, the top sanctioning body in the Midwest for late model stock cars.

Even WIR, which takes elaborate safety precautions and which has never had a fatal stock car accident in its 19-year existence, came under question.

There were suspicions – both untrue – that the track had been asked before to correct the guardrail where Detjens crashed, and that WIR was not equipped to deal with an injury as serious as his.

In response to the speculation surrounding Detjens' death, the *Press-Gazette* has interviewed nearly two dozen people to get the answers to the following questions:

What happened in the Detjens crash?
Why did it happen?
What are the after-effects of the fatal crash on the racing community?

The crash: Kulwicki and Detjens were running on the 14th lap of the feature race. They came out of Turn 2 high on the track when the accident happened.

Kulwicki, who said he was traveling more than 100 miles per hour, was against the outside wall with Detjens just inside of him. They had already straightened out at the head of the backstretch when their cars touched. "His right front tire rubbed my left rear," said Kulwicki. "It wasn't hardly a bump. It just started out as a minor bump to have the consequences it did. Guys rub tires and bump into each other all the time.

"And usually by that point down the backstretch, you're going straight. It's when you least expect it (contact) to happen."

Kulwicki corrected his skid. He didn't know that Detjens was in serious trouble. "I got back in the pits and started thinking about getting my car back in the race," he said. "I asked someone, 'How bad is he?' They said, 'His arm's cut real bad and he might lose part of his arm.' Then I really started feeling sick. I just lost my drive to compete and left the track. I never needed any escort.

"I left that night feeling badly and just praying to God that that he'd retain his arm," said Kulwicki. "Then I read in the paper the next morning that he'd died, and I was shocked. But I don't feel guilty. I don't feel I did anything wrong. I know I gave him plenty of room to get through that turn. I would say I held my line. But I don't even want to speculate that he did anything wrong. It was just one of those things."

Bill Gronley of ARTGO was flagman for the race. "I consider it strictly a racing accident," said Gronley, choosing his words carefully. "We don't like the contact, but that type is a very incidental type, not a major type. I think it takes very little movement of a car. Six inches to a foot of movement causes this thing.

"But I believe there was this type of movement off the wall by Alan's car. I don't think he made the movement to crowd. But he made the movement away from the wall and he made the movement too far. But there's no question in my mind that it was strictly a racing accident. At this point, I just feel very, very sorry for Alan. I respect his ability and I know how he's taking it."

Driver Wayne Roffers of Oneida, who was running third, said the touch happened too quickly to see. "I couldn't point a finger at either one of them," said Roffers, whose racer became tangled up in the crash. "But I will say that Larry got tail-loose out of (Turn) Two a couple of times (on earlier laps) while he was running second to Kulwicki."

Veteran driver Dick Trickle, a close friend of Detjens, was further back on the track and had no view of the touch. "I'm kind of the old dad of racing, so Alan called me up after this and we talked," said Trickle. "And I don't think Alan did anything wrong."

Said Roffers: "What Alan thought happened should be good enough."

It's good enough for Kathy Detjens, Larry's widow.

"He didn't cause Larry's death," she said last week. "You can't hold something like that against him. I hope that doesn't affect him and I hope he can go on racing."

She told Kulwicki that when he attended her husband's funeral.

"It meant a lot to me," said Kulwicki. "I know I'm square with the people who count."

The guardrail

After the touch, Detjens slid out of control far down the track toward the infield.

"A lot of us do touch coming out of that corner," said driver J.J. Smith of Appleton. "But to have it slide that far, all the way down the chute – it was just really strange."

It was later learned that Detjens' right front tire may have blown or been slashed from the contact with Kulwicki's car. This may explain why he couldn't steer out of his skid.

Still going sideways, Detjens' car struck the unprotected end of a steel guardrail at the opening to the pit opening near Turn 3.

"He struck the guardrail with his right front corner of his car," said ARTGO's McKarns. "It caused the car to spin around so that the passenger door slid into the guardrail."

What happened next is so unusual that Outagamie County Coroner Phil

Russell said he spent three days trying "to put it right in my mind."

Detjens' car hit the endpost so hard that it pushed the steel rail back like an accordion. A few feet in from the endpost, the rail bowed together like a knife-like projection. The right side of Detjens' car then spun against this point.

Russell said this bowed point struck the car's lower right corner by the back wheel and came up through. It hit Detjens' pelvic area, severed his right arm and then passed in front of him, hitting the inside of the driver's door. "If it had been two feet either way, he'd be alive today," said Russell.

"This guardrail just finds its way through the car and finds its target," said Ron Wimmer, Detjens' brother-in-law and crew member. As the car continued to slide to a stop, the guardrail withdrew "like a needle," said Wimmer.

The guardrail, then, was not in Detjens' car when he stopped. "In no way was he trapped in the wreckage," said ARTGO's McKarns.

Since the accident, WIR has angled the back pit entrance guardrail back a few feet off the track. It also anchored a bumper stand of tires in front of the endpost. "It'd be pretty hard to get a car in the guardrail the way they got it now," said Roffers.

Why hadn't the guardrail been changed before? "There was never no question on it," said track manager Roger Van Daalwyk of Kaukauna, whose father Joe owns the track.

"That guardrail never really bothered me," said driver Rich Somers, a view shared by several drivers. "During the racing, it's something you never saw."

Smith, however, had noticed it. He brought up the topic a couple of years ago at a Fox River Racing Club meeting. The club, which leases WIR for its Thursday night race programs, meets monthly in the off-season. Among other things, it discusses possible track improvements.

Smith wanted to close down the back pit entrance and double up the traffic on the front stretch pit entrance. "But it (a single pit entrance) makes for a lot more confusion," said Smith. "We looked at it (the guardrail) a few times and it looked like no way anything serious would happen out of it."

There was just mild discussion. The topic was never presented to the Van Daalwyks. "We all thought it was safe," said Smith. "We looked at it and we *knew* it was safe."

Larry Detjens at WIR in 1974.
(Pete Vercauteren photo)

Rescue personnel

The WIR always has one, and usually two ambulances at every event, said track safety director Tom Schmit, a paramedic who has been at WIR for 15 years.

There are two paramedics with each ambulance. One unit is parked near the east end of the track, the other near the pit entrance at the west end where Detjens hit.

A safety truck, with three fire trained men, is also present, Schmit said. And because the Aug. 1 program was an ARTGO program, McKarns had one of his safety trucks at the track, too. The ARTGO truck and Schmit's ambulance were parked a few feet from the Detjens end rail hit.

Schmit estimates that it took less than 10 minutes to get the car roof off and cut through the one roll bar above Detjens' head.

He and his paramedics then went to work bandaging Detjens' arm and setting up an I.V., which took about another five minutes, said Schmit. It was obvious to him that Detjens had critical internal injuries and possibly some spinal injuries.

To keep his injured internal areas immobile, it was necessary to strap Detjens to a backboard. This painstaking process took about 15 minutes.

Some bystanders in the pits who couldn't see the paramedics working inside the car, wondered why Detjens wasn't just pulled through the roof immediately. "If we hadn't put this board on him, he probably would have died before we got him out of the car," said Schmit.

As a precaution, a backup ambulance had been summoned from Appleton. It arrived just as the paramedics were removing Detjens from the car. Some witnesses mistakenly thought the WIR paramedics spent the last 15 minutes just waiting for the other ambulance.

Detjens was taken to St. Elizabeth Hospital in Appleton where he was pronounced dead at 9:24 p.m., about an hour after the crash. Coroner Russell said the cause of death was massive internal injuries.

The track

Detjens' death was the first stock car fatality at WIR since it opened in 1963. The only other fatality there involved a rocket go kart driver in 1977, said WIR public relations director Gary Vercauteren.

Vercauteren pointed to a state record 137 drivers who competed in a recent WIR Thursday night program. "Obviously, they wouldn't race if it wasn't safe," he said.

The track is insured by K&K Insurance All-Risk Insurance Company of Fort Wayne, Indiana. A spokesman for the firm believes it has insured WIR "since its existence." K&K inspects the track yearly along guidelines set up by the insurance industry, which the spokesman wouldn't specify.

But if a track is marginal, K&K won't insure it even for a higher premium. "It either meets the criteria to be insured or it doesn't," said the spokesman. "But I will say this. That particular facility (the WIR) is a very well run facility."

Conclusions

The WIR safety record through the years has been good. It shares the credit for that with the Fox River Racing Club.

Three years ago, WIR replaced the inner front stretch guardrail with a concrete wall. For this season an unneeded stretch of guardrail between Turns 1 and 2 was removed.

Early this year the exposed endpost where the rail resumed near Turn 2 was sloped into the ground. After Detjens' Aug. 1 crash, it was buried deeper.

So safety has been a continuous concern.

But as Detjens crew member Scott Maves said, "Sure you can say there's only been one (stock car) fatality. But go around the pits and ask the drivers, and they'd say that's one fatality too many."

Since Detjens' death, the drivers have started taking long-shot hazards seriously.

Smith and Miller are disturbed by a guardrail overlapped improperly on the west end of the track. "The chances are remote, they say, but if it hit the wrong way it could swing out and slice a car.

Roffers said the pit exit coming out of Turn 4 offers a concrete wall which "A person could get into trouble. I missed it by about 10 feet this year. If somebody takes a timeout and just looks around, maybe they'll find some more. And maybe at a lot of other tracks, too. There are other bad spots in other race tracks around the area in general."

"This winter at the racing club meetings, there will be quite a bit of discussion about safety," predicted Vercauteren.

That apparently sits well with WIR Manager Roger Van Daalwyk. "In order to have a fast track, you have to have a safe track," he said.

A fast track, of course, lures race fans.

The WIR is nearing the end of its most successful season. An average of 4,600 fans have attended the regular Thursday night stock car shows. Season attendance for both stock and drag racing programs at its adjoining drag strip stands at more than 108,000.

With seven events left, Vercauteren says final attendance will be about 125,000 – compared to the previous record of 111,000 in 1979. "WIR is a very prosperous track," said McKarns.

So the funds for minor improvements – at least at WIR – are there. "But there are some things the owner just doesn't see," said Smith.

Who should do the seeing?

Insurance companies like K&K inspect, but don't make suggestions.

The only state which inspects race tracks is New Jersey, said Maves, the Detjens crew member.

Many racing people don't think outside regulation is the answer.

"I think it should be done individually," said driver Miller. He said McKarns, with the weight of ARTGO's 150 drivers behind him, could put considerable influence on tracks to fine-tune their ovals.

McKarns says ARTGO has rejected tracks with obvious hazards. But he plans to sit down this winter with drivers like Miller to discuss track safety.

Ultimately, said Miller, "I think it's up to the drivers."

Drivers have always been preoccupied with making their cars safe. But they know the risks involved in their sport. They are at the mercy of a machine malfunction like a stuck throttle.

That's why a lot of drivers are fatalistic.

But track hazards, no matter how trivial or innocent looking, aren't planned by fate. They are manmade. They can be changed, if someone identifies them and speaks out.

Otherwise, even the safest car is vulnerable.

"It (Detjens' accident) could have happened somewhere else, Greensboro or Dallas," said Miller. "And it will, unless some of these things are taken care of."

"There shouldn't even be that chance," said Wimmer. "Even if it's one-in-a-million."

It would take very little effort or money say, to identify and bury an exposed endpost.

How much easier that would be than having to bury another driver like Larry Detjens?

"If Larry's death means anything, I hope it means improved safety at short tracks all over the country. I just feel very badly that one of my best friends had to die so that the rest of us wake up."

-Driver Mike Miller

Alan Kulwicki in 1979. (Pete Vercauteren photo)

Alan Kulwicki/Mike Randerson
Potent Duo

It was during a rainout late in the 1979 season when Mike Randerson first met Alan Kulwicki.

The Thursday night races had gotten rained out at Wisconsin International Raceway. Randerson, who was in the process of transforming his business, RanderCar Racing in Appleton, from a part-time gig to a full-time operation, was working with Gary Roehborn in his shop one evening when Kulwicki popped in unannounced.

"Gary was my only full-time employee then," recalled Randerson. "We were putting a new tail section on a race car and all of a sudden Alan shows up at our shop – out of the blue – with his race car on a trailer in my driveway."

Randerson knew who Kulwicki was. The Greenfield driver and University of Wisconsin-Milwaukee mechanical engineering graduate had been racing on the dirt at Leo's Speedway in Oshkosh and would eventually win the 1979 Fox River Racing Club late model title at WIR.

"Gary and I knew who he was and we both knew he showed a lot of promise," Randerson said. "He had run real well in '79, and that's even with some real tough competition on Thursday nights."

Kulwicki was driving a car built by Greg Krueger out of Milwaukee.

"Greg didn't have any interest in continuing with the stock car building business, as he was more of a modified builder as I recall," said Randerson. "So Greg told me he was going to send any of his customers my way. That's how Alan showed up by us."

Kulwicki sized up Randerson's operation, and he chatted with Randerson and Roehborn about what his plans were for the 1980 season.

"Alan was a true one-man show," explained Randerson. "He was his own engineer. He was his own P.R. man. He went out and aggressively got sponsors and he tried to be his own mechanic."

With the help of Milwaukee-area businessmen Terry Jeffords and Ed Cluka, Kulwicki landed radio station WLPX -97 out of Milwaukee as a title sponsor. While Kulwicki waited to firm up some sponsorship commitments in October and November, RanderCar Racing experienced a growth spurt as Randerson and Roehborn continued to build new cars and repair existing ones for their customers.

"Finally, in November, Alan was able to secure the funding from WLPX and other sponsors for 1980 and we started putting a car together for him," said Randerson.

The month of December rolled around, and out of the blue Kulwicki dropped sort a bombshell on Randerson and Roehborn.

"(Alan) says to me, 'Mike, I've got to have this car done in time for the World of Wheels show at State Fair Park.' " Randerson shrugged his shoulders and thought, "No problem." There was a slight problem, however. The car show was slated for January of 1980!

"In short, we worked through the Christmas holiday and weekends and nights to get that car done," said Randerson.

Even Randerson's wife, Phyllis, lent a hand whenever she could. The car was finished in the nick of time for the World of Wheels show in January.

Kulwicki raced for a living in 1980, running weekly at WIR on Thursday nights and on Sunday nights at Slinger Speedway north of Milwaukee.

"Alan would also cherry-pick some specials with our car and he was able to obtain enough sponsor dollars where he could afford to make a go of it," said Randerson. "His ultimate goal was to get to the ASA circuit the following year and then on to NASCAR."

In addition to the car Kulwicki raced for Randerson, he went down south to NASCAR car builder Banjo Matthews.

"Alan, with his wheeling and dealing, had Tom Hanley of Dousman bankroll the car to run NASCAR's late model series that was down south back then," said Randerson.

The southern racing community had a field day with a driver from Wisconsin with a funny Polish name.

"I remember *Circle Track* magazine made a joke of it," said Randerson. "They had a picture of a guy holding a pit board up with the name "KULWICKI," and it said below the picture, 'What kind of a name is that for a NASCAR driver?'"

Kulwicki was known as a stickler for details during his Winston Cup and even his short track career. He expected nothing but the best effort and performance from not only himself, but his pit crew. As a result, Kulwicki often had trouble keeping crew members.

"It got to the point Gary (Roehborn) and I were wondering, 'How in the world are we going to get this car done?'" said Randerson. "I remember Gary and Alan were putting a steering column in his car. Gary was tach-welding a bracket on to hold in the steering shaft. Alan wanted him to move it over one-sixteenth of an inch. Gary yelled at him, 'You can't move that thing over one-sixteenth of an inch,' and they argued about it. They were going back and forth. Alan was ever so particular about those kind of things."

Kulwicki's attention to detail paid off as he won the opening night late model feature at WIR.

"It was a rough year though, because we wound up putting seven different front clips on that car with all the wrecks he had," said Randerson. "But most of those wrecks happened at Slinger. It wasn't uncommon for Alan's car to show up on his trailer in my driveway either late Sunday nights or early Monday mornings all crashed up. It was quite a year. We had a lot of fun. We did a lot of experimenting."

Randerson describes Kulwicki's personality as a true Jekyll and Hyde.

"When it was time to race, he was all business and was a true taskmaster,"

Mike Randerson looks through some classic photos during a 2016 visit to WIR. (Ron Nikolai photo)

said Randerson. "When it was race day, it was like a switch flipped on and he had a game face on. He really came down hard on people when they'd made mistakes."

The duo kept meticulous notes that season.

"We'd even have a debriefing session after every race," explained Randerson. "When most teams had the coolers out and were cracking beers, we were analyzing many parts of the car and recording data and recapping how the night went and what we could have done better."

The two would often meet in the middle when it came to race car setups and such. You had two men from two opposite ends of the spectrum. Kulwicki with his book smarts and mechanical engineering degree from UW-M, and Randerson, an old-school, hands-on type who grew up on a farm in Freedom.

"Some nights we'd wring our hands over a half turn on a screw jack," said Randerson. "We were always splitting hairs it seemed. But it worked."

Randerson walked a very fine line in the pits on Thursday nights in his role as a car builder for more drivers than just Kulwicki.

"I had other customers to service, so I had to be real careful from a political standpoint so people didn't think I was putting all of my time and effort into Alan Kulwicki," explained Randerson. "Bear in mind I wanted to grow my business. Alan used me and my business as a tool to further his career, but in a way I was also doing the same to build up my business as well."

At times, Kulwicki would test Randerson's patience.

"Alan was constantly on the telephone and this was in a time when we didn't have cell phones," said Randerson. "I'd yell at him and say, 'Alan, put the damned phone down. We've got work to do.' I later realized that being on that phone constantly was a necessary thing for him. He truly was a one-man band. He was constantly lining up sponsors and interviews with the media, and always putting deals together to field his rides. He was a P.R. man way ahead of his time in 1980, and in my opinion doesn't get near enough credit for that aspect of his career."

On one particularly hot Thursday afternoon in July of 1980, Kulwicki sent Randerson over the edge.

"I remember we were busier than heck in the shop and it was hot – real hot," recalled Randerson. "I remember this hot sun was just blazing. We had just put another new front clip on the car as Alan crashed the week before. We had so many cars in our shop we had to set Alan's car up in my driveway. We're so swamped and we're running late. It's looking like not only were we going to miss practice, we very well would miss time trials. So here I see Alan and Gary walking out to the driveway with a full length piece of tubing. I asked Alan, 'What are you going to do with that tubing?' Alan said, 'I don't think this driveway is flat. I want to determine the pitch of the driveway and I want to determine what the effect it will have on the caster angle setting.'"

Sweating profusely in the summer heat and humidity, Randerson finally lost it. That evening, they showed up too late to WIR for any hot laps, but nonetheless Kulwicki was able to nab fast time with a car sporting a rebuilt front clip.

At the end of the 1980 season, Kulwicki beat out another future NASCAR driver – Ted Musgrave of Grand Marsh – to win the Fox River Racing Club title. Back then it wasn't uncommon for an "outsider" who didn't live in the Fox Valley area to get shunned or roughed up on the track by the other competitors. With Kulwicki, this was not the case.

"I think the guys he raced with on Thursday nights figured it out pretty early that he was a cut above the rest," said Randerson. "I think in the end, they probably figured they could end up learning something from him. They looked up to him, in part because he was very dedicated."

Another of Randerson's family members who got to know Kulwicki quite well was Randerson's wife, Phyllis. The late nights that ensued from Kulwicki driving up from Milwaukee to work on the car frequently meant he would eat dinner with the Randersons.

"Alan wasn't real sociable, but he was just very focused," said Phyllis. "People sometimes mistook that for arrogance. He was just that driven. He really became sort of a member of our family that year. Later that winter, we went to Florida. Alan drove us to the airport. He was real sick. We came back a week later and Alan is still sick. I told Alan he needed to take some vitamins. He couldn't just get some vitamin C or anything without researching it thoroughly. Three of our kids have red hair. He asked me, dead seriously one day, 'If I take these vitamins, will my hair turn red?'

"That was probably the lightest I'd ever seen Alan. He did talk a little bit about his family right after Christmas that winter. He was really very guarded and rarely talked about family. He was very cautious about his feelings."

With the 1980 season behind them, both Kulwicki and Randerson had plans to be involved in the ASA circuit.

"From a business standpoint, I felt I needed to be visible in ASA," said Randerson. "At the end of 1980, Alan and I went over to Ed Howe in Beaverton, Michigan, and got some stuff. I was a Howe dealer at the time. We met Mark Martin in 1980. He was running a Dillion car. He and Mark Martin got a relationship. He took Alan under his wing from a setup standpoint. It was all welded together. The pair brought the car home and we did our own thing to it."

With Kulwicki's stock rising in the local and regional racing ranks, he was able to garner show money on occasion, often for John McKarns ARTGO series races in 1981.

"He would cherry-pick some of those specials," said Randerson.

One of those specials was on August 1, 1981. ARTGO hosted a Saturday night venue at WIR with twin 50-lap features on tap. Wausau's Larry Detjens was one of the winningest short track drivers in the Midwest.

"Larry started out that year in New Smyrna Beach, Florida, at Speedweeks with a Frings-built car and he was wicked fast," recalled Randerson. "He was winning darn near every night. He flew back on the same plane as my wife and I to take part in a ski meet at Rib Mountain, so he just up and left Speedweeks early that year. He was one of the fastest cars every night there. But he also loved to ski."

After Detjens had piled up several wins in the Frings car, he crashed badly and eventually switched back to a Bemco car, built by Bill Bembinster from Detjens' hometown of Wausau.

That August 1 race would be the last of Detjens' life.

"Alan and Larry were both racing way hard for that early in the race, at least that's always been my opinion," recalled Randerson. "I think they both felt if they could get the lead in that race, they could run their own line. I was also helping Wayne Roffers that night. Wayne was running third behind those two and his car was really fast. In fact, Wayne was just waiting for those guys to sort out – he was running half throttle.

"Coming out of turn two, Alan and Larry were racing hard. Alan was on the inside and Larry was in the outer groove. They made contact and Larry lost control and started spinning. He just would not put (the car) around. He tried and tried to save it. He counter steered and counter steered to try and save it. But he just couldn't save it."

Detjens car spun on the backstretch, his car slicing into the pit entrance retaining guardrail heading into turn three. The guardrail threaded through Detjens' car, and the car bounced around and the guardrail withdrew from the car like a needle. Detjens was cut badly and suffered massive internal injuries that ultimately caused his death.

"If you tried one million times to replicate what happened with his car that night, you couldn't," said Randerson. "That deal was a total fluke, a freak thing."

Randerson was among the many on hand who worked to extricate Detjens from the car.

"Bill (Bembinster) was in there helping, too, and we knew before we left that night that Larry didn't make it," said Randerson. "Alan didn't finish the race that night. He did have some damage to his car and he loaded up and left.

In my opinion, part of the reason I think Larry raced so hard that night was he had a push in the car. He knew if he would have gotten in traffic he would have likely went backwards."

Kulwicki went home and later learned of Larry's passing.

"Alan was devastated to say the least," said Randerson. "A few guys from Central Wisconsin were shooting their mouths off that night saying stuff like, 'We'll get Kulwicki,' and truly it wasn't his fault. It was a racing deal. But Larry was their friend. Looking back now I can understand how they felt at the time."

Kulwicki did get some reassurance of sorts when he got a call from Dick Trickle a day or two after the crash.

"Alan asked Dick, 'Am I running you guys too hard?'" said Randerson. "Trickle said, 'Yes, but it's nothing we can't handle.' He was down in the dumps, but to hear Trickle reassure him seemed to help.

"Alan asked me, 'Should I go to that funeral?' I told him, 'Absolutely.' He did. When he went there, at first they may have looked at him funny. But eventually they had a change of heart."

On the way home from Detjens' funeral, Kulwicki stopped by Randerson's shop.

"We had a long heart-to-heart conversation the night of Larry's funeral and he told me, 'I'm sure glad I went.' He had to go on. He couldn't carry that with him. As Alan's career blossomed, it was never mentioned very often. It was a heat-of-the-battle deal."

"I've worked with drivers who were dedicated to racing, but not in the same way as Alan. They weren't all-in like he was. Racing was an obsession with Alan. We had Ted Musgrave, Jim Sauter and Dick Trickle, and Marzofka, Reffner, Back, etc. If you look at Alan's natural ability, he had less natural ability than any of those guys. With his obsession and dedication, he took his engineering things and put it to good use. We met in the middle on things more so than people realized. He applied practical application to things. Alan literally taught himself how to get better and better. It was continually a learning process with him. It never stopped."

As the years went on, Kulwicki was his own boss, owning his own team in NASCAR and racing on his own dime in Winston Cup.

"We stayed in regular contact with Alan when he moved down south," said Randerson. "It was 1986 and it was his first year in NASCAR. He had sponsorship from Quincy's Steakhouse. He was telling me how he was working out of this shop that had no insulation or air conditioning. He said it was really, really hot down there. But he was determined to keep going."

Years had gone by and Randerson had sold the business to his nephew Jim Randerson.

"After I went to work for Oshkosh Truck in 1992, (Alan) won the Winston Cup championship," said Randerson. "My phone rang at my desk. It was Alan. We had a very long talk. He thanked me for all I've done with him. We had a great conversation."

That was the last time Randerson ever talked to Kulwicki.

Kulwicki died in an airplane crash on Thursday, April 1, 1993. He was returning from an appearance at the Knoxville Hooters in a Hooters corporate plane on a short flight across Tennessee before the Sunday spring race at Bristol Motor Speedway. The plane slowed and crashed just before final approach at Tri-Cities Regional Airport near Blountville. The National Transportation Safety Board attributed the crash to the pilot's failure to use the airplane's anti-ice system. Kulwicki was just thirty-eight years old.

In the end, Kulwicki ultimately did things his way.

Al Golueke in 1976. (Pete Vercauteren photo)

Al Golueke
Shop Rat

As a student at Green Bay East High School in the early 1970s, Al Golueke was a self-admitted "shop rat." He spent most of his elective courses and study hall times in the machine and power mechanics shops.

"My friends and I were race car nuts growing up, and we devoured those hot rod magazines that were popular then," said Golueke. "We were lucky to catch a fifteen-minute segment of a race on *Wide World of Sports* back then. That's about all the coverage the sport got back then."

Golueke got exposed to the sport of speed first hand as a youngster in 1969.

"My buddy's name was John Schultz," recalled Golueke. "One day, Mr. Schultz, his dad, asked me if I'd like to tag along with them to the races at De Pere. John and I piled in the back of his dad's really cool Mustang, and off to De Pere we went."

He was hooked from the moment he first walked up the ramp underneath the grandstands of the track located at the Brown County Fairgrounds to their seats.

"What drew me to oval track racing was the action never stopped," said Golueke. "It was totally different than drag racing. I soaked in the sights and the smells of gear lube. It was addicting right from the start."

Once the final checkered flag flew that night, Mr. Schultz suggested they go down into the pit area and see the cars and meet the drivers.

"That's the first time I met Red BeDell," Golueke said. "I mean, the races were done, but here was this guy, in a racing suit that looked like he hadn't even raced in it. He was smiling and handing out racing stickers to all the kids who surrounded him. He had the big hauler with the Confederate flag and his convertible race car that just looked so cool. That was it for me. I decided I wanted to be part of this thing called motorsports."

Gene Bray was the football coach and industrial arts teacher at East High.

"One day, (Mr. Bray) had me and my buddy, Bruce Charlier, grab some torches and go cut up an old seven-man football (blocking) sled at the edge of the practice field near the East River," said Golueke. "We salvaged some of the metal parts from that sled as I figured out I could use some of that metal when it came to building the roll cage for my race car. We saw opportunities as we were cutting it up that sled."

With his eye on racing the following year, Golueke began scouring the local newspapers and found a 1956 Chevy for sale in Mill Center in rural Brown County.

"I called the guy and asked about it, and my dad (Nick Golueke) and I drove out there," he said.

Al Golueke pulled $45 out of his wallet he had earned from one of his multiple paper routes. He was now the proud owner of a street car that would later be converted into a race car.

"The thing was stuck up to the hub caps in mud," recalled Golueke. "We spent a whole afternoon with bumper jacks and some wood. We wound up towing it with a chain all the way back home to Allouez. By the time we hit the Walnut Street bridge, smoke was rolling out from under the fenders. We made it home on a hope and a prayer."

Golueke bought a six-cylinder motor in Pulaski from Gil Wagner for $75.

"The irony was Gil and his brother, Russ, were going to race at WIR and they were pulling the six-cylinder motor out and putting in a V-8 to race with," said Golueke. "And I was getting their discarded motor and I was going to race with that smaller six-cylinder motor."

The garage Golueke worked in during the summer of '74 was hot and muggy. He did not have the luxury of power tools, not even a cutting torch.

"I did buy a welder, but all of that piping was cut with a hacksaw," Golueke pointed out. "It was a very slow process, but eventually I got it done."

Golueke's father was a photographer by trade for Stiller Photography in Green Bay.

"Every couple of days, Dad would come out and snap some photos of the car in different stages of progression, so I have a virtual time frame of the building of the car, which is pretty cool," said Golueke.

When it was all said and done, Golueke had roughly $600 invested in his straight six-powered '56 Chevy. It was complete with his street-legal tires he bought from Fleet Farm. With Kaukauna not set to open until June 12, 1975, Golueke was all revved up with no place to race in May of that year.

"My buddy, Pete Bushmaker, stopped over one day and asked me, 'When are you gonna race this thing?' " said Golueke. "He said, 'What about racing at De Pere?' They had started a hobby stock class that year. So it was pretty neat. My first-ever race was actually at De Pere. I was the slowest car out there all day. I passed one guy when he dropped out. But I was making laps and was thrilled to be part of it."

A couple of weeks later, Golueke made his debut at WIR on a cold, rainy day.

"We actually raced in the mist that day," said Golueke. "I was new and got my feet wet during the year and learned each week."

Golueke crashed hard into the concrete wall during an end-of-the-year special at WIR that year. The car was bent so badly he couldn't even tow it home.

"The track wrecker operator volunteered to tow my car back home for me nearly thirty miles," he said. "That's the spirit of camaraderie we had back then. Everyone just helped out one another."

While attempting to get his race car back into shape, Golueke crossed paths with Mike Schmelzer, owner of Bay Speed Center.

Al Golueke in the early 1980s. (Pete Vercauteren photo)

"Mike loaned me some tools to get my car fixed, and we basically struck a deal on tuning up that six-cylinder motor to squeeze more horsepower out of it," said Golueke. That started a friendship between the two that lasted through the decades. "The jist of the deal was if I did most of the work and paid for all the parts, they'd help me out a little bit with the machining work and stuff with that six-cylinder motor. We raced the same car in '76, and ran with somewhat of a souped-up motor."

With Golueke running a six-cylinder against the V-8s, it was almost like bringing a knife to a gun fight. After the 1976 season, Golueke built a '72 Chevelle and evolved into a front-running car in what was quickly becoming a very competitive sportsman class.

"Paul Jochman and Pete Berken were real tough then," recalled Golueke. "We even had some guys come down from Menominee, Michigan, who were tough by the names of Rick Collar and Donny Anderson. They were great guys and fun to race against."

It was in 1977 when the young, ambitious and very wide-eyed Golueke stepped to the plate and served as vice president for the FRRC.

"Rene Grode and Ron Van Roy talked me into stepping up," said Golueke. "Looking back, I might have been the only hand that went up to volunteer for it. I really wanted to get involved with things. What I recall the most about those days is it was an all-for-one-and-one-for-all mentality – a true spirit of cooperation. We went to a point where we were without a place to race when Apple Creek closed down after 1974 and we were just happy to have a place to race. We didn't have trouble getting people to step up and help. Nowadays it's different. The drivers want to just sit back and complain about things all the time. It wasn't quite so bad back then."

Golueke decided to step down at the end of his two-year term.

"I was running up front more, and in my mind there was a conflict with me serving as a club officer and a racer," said Golueke.

Golueke won the sportsman track championship against some tough competition in 1979.

"I sold the car to Steve Giese and went to work building a late model chassis I acquired from Bay Speed Center," said Golueke, who even then bucked the trend of buying the hottest and newest trick chassis off the showroom floor. "The Howe and Dillion chassis were selling very well, but I still preferred to build my own cars."

The tedious process of building his own race car prevented Golueke from getting in much racing during 1980.

"I made it out the last night of the year in 1980 and ran for rookie-of-the-year and won it in 1981," said Golueke. "I beat out Bruce Bares from Belgium to win it."

Golueke got a late start on his 1982 season, as he was out of work for a bit after the business he was working at closed their doors.

"When I did come back, I had car number 28, as did Jim Weber and Jerry Schneider, and all three of us were in the same class," said Golueke. "One night after the races, we were having a few cold ones at the Corner Pub and Weber says to me, 'One of us has to change our car number,' because for a while they were getting our lineups confused with the duplicate numbers. So I switched to number 82."

Golueke began spreading his wings in the mid-1980s, running at 141 Speedway's paved oval in Francis Creek on Saturday nights.

"Guys who ran the sportsman class didn't care about running for points at 141 on Saturday nights," said Golueke. "Guys would run the tires they ran Thursday nights at WIR on Saturday nights at 141, so guys weren't spending a lot of money then on Saturday nights. 141 was pretty much a stress-free deal. I still ran WIR once in a while and won the Budweiser 500 in the fall of 1986 at WIR."

Golueke parted out his asphalt car in 1987 and switched to the dirt, purchasing a modified from Dave Mueller at Cobra chassis and running at Luxemburg Speedway.

"The IMCA modified was very new at the time locally, and I was serving as the pit steward at Seymour Speedway," recalled Golueke. "I did a lot of stuff with Kelly Hafeman, who was tough in an IMCA modified in the early years."

Golueke, who always had a passion for working on carburetors, developed a product called a "carb hat" after his racing days, which took off well. Since then, he's continued to build and rebuild carburetors for many Midwestern drivers. The business is called Carbs by Al Golueke. He continues to toy with carburetors to this day.

"That lets me still be involved with this sport in some capacity," he said.

Larry Schuler was one of a dedicated group of drivers over the years who traveled long distances to race at WIR. (Pete Vercauteren photo)

The Long Haulers
Windshield Time

Over the decades, there have been a handful of teams who have gone the extra mile to compete on Thursday nights at Wisconsin International Raceway. Whether they trekked from south of the border in Illinois to the north from Michigan's Upper Peninsula, or even from the west and the land of 10,000 lakes in Minnesota, some teams put in a lot of extra windshield time in order to turn some laps on the D-shaped, half-mile. Here are the stories of some of those drivers.

"The Junkyard Dog"
Larry Schuler – Minooka, Illinois

Larry Schuler admits, "I'm not sure exactly how we pulled it off back then."

Schuler, now age sixty-three, made the grueling four-hour and fifteen-minute trek north to Kaukauna on Thursday nights from 1975 to 1977, not missing a Thursday night. Schuler worked as a linemen for Illinois Bell as he says "climbing poles and digging holes." When he'd clock out early on Thursdays at 3:30 p.m. at his worksite – wherever that might be in suburban Chicagoland – Schuler hopped in his rig and headed north on Highway 41 – which back then was only two lanes for much of the stretch.

"Dad (Lee Schuler) and my brother (Tracy Schuler) would leave ahead of time to tow the car up there and I'd usually get in there barely in time to time trial," said Schuler. "I would almost never have time to practice the car at all. Just hop in and go."

The FRRC had started up the Thursday night weekly program in 1975 and was in desperate need of cars. Despite being well over four hours away, the Schuler family was happy to oblige.

"We were always treated very well by the people up there," said Schuler, who won the 1976 late model title. "The folks up there were always very professional. When you're from out of town, sometimes you're not always as welcome as you think you should be. We had nothing but a great experience up there – we were treated like gold.

"I guess we got caught up in the enthusiasm for the place. It was unique, too. All the corners of the track were different. It was fun to race."

Traffic jams were common during the long commute over three seasons, as were mechanical failures.

Schuler said, "I remember one time we were four or five miles down the road on Highway 55. I was coming up from work. I saw my dad was pulled over on the side of the road. They had a rusty fuel tank in the hauler and the truck quit running. So they backed the car off the trailer and drove the car right to the track on Highway 55, right through town. They got some real funny looks. I took the helmet and borrowed an air gauge and a jack, and went out and qualified. The guys at the gate gave me a hard time. But we made it to the track, and barely on time."

Lee Schuler had a solid friendship with George Appleton of Appleton Rack and Pinion, a race car parts supplier in Chicagoland. "George was buddies with Lynn Blanchard up in the Kaukauna area and they got along great," said Schuler. "That was another reason we came up was Lynn. He was a great motor man. Back in '70's I was working on two different cars. It made it tough because Friday nights we'd run Grundy (County Speedway in

Morris, Illinois – his home track). It was a busy time in our lives."

The nickname "Junkyard Dog" came from the fact that several of the parts on Schuler's racers came straight from the junkyard.

"Everybody was tough at WIR," recalled Schuler. "I remember going wheel-to-wheel with guys like Pete Parker, Willie Goeden, Roger Regeth and JJ Smith. Rich Somers was a champion one year. Wally Jors was a Howe chassis dealer up there. He was a good man who died way too young. Those guys were great to race with."

Schuler also got to be friends with Kiel's Dale Koehler, who raced late model and had run some USAC stock car races over the years.

"Dale had a bar and grill in Kiel, and we'd stop there on the way home to get a quick sandwich for the road," said Schuler. "He'd manage to get back ahead of us somehow. We got fed and got out of there. He wasn't somebody I ran up against every week, but he was a great guy to talk to. I'd still go to work Friday mornings, sometimes on only two hours of sleep. You wound up learning how to sleep fast. Some nights, a couple of hours of sleep seemed fast. We didn't stay around drinking much or anything. We had to get loaded up and got home. The Port Washington police stopped me a couple of times. They weren't too happy with me speeding home sometimes."

In 1976, Schuler pulled off an amazing feat – winning late model titles in three states all in the same year: Thursday nights at WIR in Kaukauna, Friday nights at Grundy County (Illinois) and Saturday nights at Illiana Motor Speedway in Schereville, Indiana.

During Schuler's dominating years in the 1970s, it was nothing for him to beat the likes of the legendary Dick Trickle, Larry Detjens or Tom Reffner.

"I learned so much racing against those guys, and in fact when I first raced with them was down in New Smyrna for Speedweeks down in Florida. What I learned the most from those guys was that you didn't have to beat and bang your way to get to the front. And that's the way you should race."

Schuler and his crew decided to pare back their schedule after 1977.

"We loved running at WIR on Thursday nights, but we started to wear our crew out," said Schuler. "And the gas prices started going up then, too. One year we ran something like eighty shows. It was too much. We still went up for the Red, White and Blue shows for a while. We've been up there since, because I help out Ricky Baker on the ARCA Midwest Tour. We were there for the Dixieland race (in 2015) and I ran into some of the same people. They are still very nice. The crowds seemed decent and they seemed full of energy."

Schuler's never kept track of his total feature wins, but he's still "got it." In 2015, Schuler won three late model features at Grundy. His car is owned by Rod Baker Ford.

"When I hot-lapped it for them, I thought I was just warming up the seat for Ricky (Baker). Come to find out they roll out a new car for me one day. As long as I have a ride, I'll keep racing. I cannot afford this on my own. It's more fun for me now just running basically one night a week."

"The Hyde Hustler"
Bob Iverson – Hyde, Michigan

Bob Iverson was inducted into Michigan's Motor Sports Hall of Fame in 2002. His numerous track titles, feature wins and track records at Norway Speedway (ten track titles) and Escanaba Raceway (seven track titles) helped earn him the title of "the best racing driver in Upper Michigan."

Iverson was fast qualifier each night of the 1982 season at Escanaba and won all of the features that year except for one. He remains the only U.P. driver to capture 100 career feature wins in a career spanning four decades. After winning pretty much all there was to win in Michigan in the early 1980s, Iverson decided to begin making the two-hour and twenty-minute trek south every Thursday night to WIR.

"We'd run the open wheel (modifieds) for a long time," Iverson pointed out. "We'd had a lot of success in our home state. When they paved Norway, I really took a liking to the asphalt and we decided to start running WIR on a weekly basis. And we were just looking for something different back then, too."

It didn't take Iverson long to develop a healthy, spirited rivalry with Green Bay's Scott Hansen, who would go on to win five straight late model championships.

"The first time I wound up racing with Scotty was actually at De Pere on the dirt," explained Iverson. "We both got involved in a pretty bad wreck there and it wasn't neither of our fault."

Hansen ditched the dirt and concentrated full time on the pavement beginning in 1983. Over the years, the pair would go toe-to-toe.

"Bob was a great guy and a great racer," said Hansen. "He'd always race me hard, but clean. I never had to worry about what Bob was going to do. We had some great battles over the years."

Said Iverson: "I know a couple of those years we'd finish second to Scott in the final point standings when it was all said and done. I'd often have more fast times and feature wins than he would, but we'd come up just short. But we got along great with him. We partied with him and his crew – drank some beers at his shop in Green Bay a couple of times."

When he wasn't racing his red Bero Motors-sponsored No. 97, Iverson drove semi-truck, hauling pulp to the paper mills for a living.

"I worked for myself, so I would often knock off work early on Thursdays," he said.

Cell phones weren't prevalent in the mid-1980s. As such, once the team hit the road, they'd often finish the trip to WIR, rain or shine.

"We got burned a few times on that, but what are you to do?" said Iverson. "Sometimes it wouldn't start raining until we hit Green Bay. But we were like, 'We've come this far, we might as well go the extra twenty miles.'"

Road construction, sometimes slowing things down to a one-lane snail's pace, would impede Iverson's team from getting to the track on time.

Iverson continued to run Norway in the mid-1980s, but after a while he curtailed running there for the "$1,000-to-win races" such as the State Line Challenge.

"I ran some of the ARTGO shows mainly in Wisconsin," said Iverson. "I didn't hit the ones they ran in Lower Michigan, though."

Iverson got to be friends with Dick Trickle.

"I loaned my car to Dick one night when he was chasing ARTGO points. He wound up ninth I think, but it kept him in the chase."

One of Iverson's biggest accomplishments at WIR was nailing down fast time on a Sunday for the Red, White and Blue series.

"It was a big deal because Trickle, Tom Reffner, Joe Shear and all those guys were there," he said. "That's when they first came out with the 9:1 compression engines. That was a big deal for us back then."

The sport has come a long way since Iverson built his own 1947 Ford

Coupe from mostly scrap parts out of the local salvage yards.

"I don't like the way they are going with these tie-down systems and the shocks on these cars," said Iverson. "I mean, they are running $1,200 shocks. With the stuff they are running, it's just way too expensive to run."

Iverson's son, Jamie, was a champion at Norway for many seasons, and his grandson, Robbie Iverson, has taken over the wheel of the familiar No. 97, marking three generations of Iversons racing. When he's not following his son and grandson in their racing exploits, Bob Iverson found one of his old modifieds and has restored it.

Mike Gardner – Gladstone, Michigan
2006 Red White and Blue champion

For Mike Gardner, it was all about how he was treated by everyone involved with WIR that made his decision to race on Thursday nights an easy one. Gardner, who traveled six hours round trip from his home in Gladstone, Michigan, competed weekly at Kaukauna from 1999 through 2013 while driving for Chase Motorsports out of Appleton.

"I didn't start racing until later in life," explained Gardner, who won several titles racing at Norway Speedway. "We used to come down and watch the Red, White and Blue races when they were still on Sundays. Roger (Van Daalwyk) was kind enough to put me, my wife Jennifer, and daughter Michelle up in the press box. That showed me the character of the people running that place. I was running street stocks at the time in Norway. Roger really sort of took us in like family."

Gardner's first race at WIR came in 1997.

"I ran one of those CWRA restrictor plate-type races, and there were a ton of cars," said Gardner. "There was a lot of competition. At Norway, it seemed Dale Peterson and I were top dogs. For a while it came down to us two and Bob (Iverson) was handing over his car to Jamie (Iverson). But when I came to WIR, there was never any guarantee we'd make the show. Not ever. We came to embrace the competition."

Gardner was fortunate in that he often had many summers off.

"I was a vocational school teacher, so for me the travel wasn't as bad," said Gardner. "My wife Jennifer was very, very supportive. There were nights we'd stay and sign autographs in the pits for the fans, and we wouldn't roll into our driveway in Michigan until 4 a.m. Still, Jennifer always made it to work every Friday by 8 a.m. no matter how late we got home from the races the night before."

The Gardners didn't have the luxury of cell phones for much of their time racing at WIR.

"Jeff Van Oudenhoven's dad, Milo, Dave Valentyne and Roger (Van Daalwyk) would often call us on the landline the minute the races rained out, and that was very cool and saved us a few trips down there," said Gardner. "We also had a few times when we towed down there with our open trailer and got rained out anyways. But that's the way it went sometimes."

Gardner worked as a mechanic a few summers.

"I worked for Bero Motors, and Larry (Bero) used to sponsor Bob (Iverson), so he'd give me Thursdays off and that helped out a lot, too," said Gardner. "I was also fortunate to have some really good sponsors along the way. Engineering Machine Products (EMP) built water pumps and different components for the auto industry. There were in Escanaba and we also had Werner Electric. We really did run our racing operation like a business."

After Gardner's last season driving for Chase Motorsports, he began getting depressed when the car wouldn't work well all the time.

"It was never the car owners. It was basically pressure I'd put on myself to win," said Gardner. "It was like an emotional roller coaster. I really had trouble handling bad nights. I mean, I'd end up on the couch eating chips and drinking Mountain Dew. It was tough. And it was then I just knew it was time for me to walk away. I just was never as fast as the other 45 (Jeff Van Oudenhoven) toward the end. It was sort of a mental thing for me. But I have no regrets. It was a great ride."

"The Barnstormer"
Jim Weber – Roseville, Minnesota

In stock car racing, the term "barnstormer" refers to a driver who will crisscross several states, racing anywhere and anywhere. Jim Weber most certainly fit the bill from the 1980s until his retirement from racing in 2006. A good chunk of Weber's racing career was centered on WIR, where he won the FRRC late model crown in 1992 and was a three-time Red, White and Blue state champion.

"Webs," as he was affectionately known, often lived out of a cube van in the summer, sometimes not going back home to the Land of 10,000 Lakes for weeks at a time.

"I remember one year we ran 110 shows back in the late 1980s," recalled Weber, now seventy-five years old. "I think only Tom Reffner had run that many nights prior to that. In between ARTGO shows and specials like the Slinger Nationals, we'd run Wednesdays at La Crosse, Thursdays at WIR, Fridays in Madison, Saturdays at the Dells, and finish it off Sundays at Slinger. When we had specials thrown in like the Dixieland on a Tuesday night, we'd darn near run every night of the week."

Weber had a couple of loyal sponsors over the years, including Clancy's Auto Sales, John J. Mayer Insurance, and B & B Race Engines. But during the meat of the racing season, he'd survive financially from race to race on his race winnings.

"I never knew what I was going to do from one day to the next," admitted Weber, who owned a construction company in Minnesota. "When things were going well with the construction company, I took off and went racing for a while. Sometimes if I didn't have an ARTGO show to run, I'd scoot back home for four or five days and take care of business."

Weber estimates he ran used tires, or "scuffs," 90 percent of the time during his racing career.

"I would go on (Dick) Trickle's tire rack and pay him a hundred dollars, and I'd take all the used tires I wanted. That lasted until I started beating him. Then he wouldn't give me his runoffs anymore."

Because Weber raced so often and was an ARTGO series regular for many years, some of the FRRC drivers resented the fact that what they termed a "professional" race car driver was going wheel-to-wheel with them on Thursday nights.

"I'd have more laps under my belt in two weeks then some of those guys had all season running one night a week at WIR," boasted Weber. "Roger (Van Daalwyk) always seemed to take pretty good care of me, but there were five or six guys at times with the club who seemed like they were out to ruin my career from time to time. We'd call WIR "Russia." I loved racing there, though. I always felt we had a real good handle on that place."

As the years wore on, Weber raced so frequently he was able to acquire product sponsorship from many racing parts manufacturers, thus cutting his operating costs.

"I'd get free body panels from Five Star Bodies and free chassis from Lefthander," said Weber. "Motors I'd get from Bruce (Mueller) at B & B and I had those Penske shocks I'd get free. It all helped cut our costs."

Weber's final race was at Oktoberfest at La Crosse in 2006.

"Trickle and I had a grudge match and I beat him," said Weber. "He said I cheated. I told him, 'I learned it from you.' I was really good friends with Dick. We raced together hundreds of time. He spun me out at Elko once. He dialed me and the flagman was going to black-flag him. He told the flagman he missed the gas pedal. The flagman bought it and never black-flagged him. Dick was pretty slick."

These days, Weber own a resort north of Brainerd in northern Minnesota.

"I still golf," said Weber, who has had some health issues in recent years including hip surgery, two knee replacements and a bout with cancer. "I even had a hole-in-one in 2015."

Scott Hansen in 1984. (Pete Vercauteren photo)

Scott Hansen
Titletown's Racing Champion

When it came to the late model class in the 1980s, it was a second-generation driver from Green Bay who took Wisconsin International Raceway's half-mile by storm.

Scott Hansen won five straight late model titles from 1985 to 1989. He was introduced to the sport of speed as a kid, tagging along with his dad, Rollie Hansen, who flagged at area dirt tracks.

"I remember a lot of Dad's flagging, and Dad had some real close calls," recalled Hansen. "My sister and I went to Luxemburg with the coupes. They had a big wreck down the front stretch. Dad flagged right on the track – that's just what they did back then. My dad's guardian angel that day was the water truck. He dove under the water truck when some race cars came barreling his way."

When Hansen decided to get into racing in 1975, he received full support from his parents, Rollie and Rose Hansen.

"They were very supportive of it, but didn't contribute at all financially – just time," said Hansen. "They let me use the garage space for the car."

The first car Hansen bought was from fellow racer Tom Steuding in Altoona, Wisconsin.

"Dad had a friend who had a plane, and we actually flew there and bought the car," recalled Hansen. "It was an old Chevelle. They put up with all of us guys coming and going at all hours of the night. They followed me around the country through all of my racing."

Hansen got his start on the dirt tracks of Northeastern Wisconsin.

"Red BeDell really helped me get started," said Hansen. "He must have saw something in me. He sold me my first-ever cheater set of tires. I guess there was a tire rule back then. Red was also the first guy to show me what stagger was when I had no clue what that was with tires."

Hansen's career started out rough. During his very first race at Seymour Speedway in 1975, Hansen crashed through the turn one guardrail and luckily wound up in an open space between two parked spectators cars.

"I remember I drove the thing back into the pit area, but the car was in pretty tough shape," said Hansen.

The learning curve was a tough one for Hansen early on. He struggled in his first two seasons in 1975 and 1976 on the half-mile dirt ovals at De Pere, Seymour and Shawano.

"Heck, I'm pretty sure on Saturday nights I made more money shooting pool at the Staircase bar in Bonduel than I normally made racing at Shawano," joked Hansen.

In 1977, Hansen's uncle, Curt Hansen, purchased a Boyce Trackburner chassis from Gene Wheeler – and then things improved. His first big win came that year with the car still in primer at Luxemburg Speedway. He won $1,000 in the Midwest Open.

"We had a big orange bus for a hauler, and the trophy was so big we had to lay it down in the hauler to bring it home," said Hansen. "We had trouble just getting to the race that day. We had to have Bob Menor, who also had a bus for a race hauler, push my bus up a hill on the highway on the way to Luxemburg. It was crazy."

Hansen began dabbling in the pavement at WIR, beginning with the Red,

White and Blue races.

"We'd race those specials, and that's how and when we got our feet wet at WIR," he explained.

Hansen would continue to play on both the dirt and asphalt up until the 1982 season. Little did he know a meeting at a carwash, of all places, would eventually give him the break he needed to go full time on the pavement.

"After the Shawano races Saturday nights, we'd bring our race car to this carwash at the corner of West Mason and Fisk streets on Green Bay's west side," said Hansen. "Steve Marler was a local insurance agent. He had sponsored some race cars and he would take his Mercedes to get it washed there. His office was by the carwash. He saw me one day and said, 'You know, I really don't like all this dirt and clay when I'm trying to wash my car. What's it going to take to keep you guys out of here?' We struck up a conversation and before you know it, my crew guy, Richie Wauters, was persistent with Steve and finally Richie convinced Steve to buy me an asphalt late model."

Hansen embarked on his first full-time season running Thursday nights at WIR in 1983.

"I can't thank Steve enough for what he did for us early on," said Hansen. "After I had run for Marler for a couple of seasons, I had an interview with Budweiser. They were looking to sponsor someone at Kaukauna. Terry Baldry had won the track championship and got the sponsorship from Pepsi. I finished second to Terry, and Budweiser wanted to sponsor someone on Thursday nights. I didn't have a car at the time.

"When they came to interview me, I had Tom Haen's car and hauler in the shop. I told them, 'This is what we have going.' Once I got the sponsor money, I turned around and bought out Bob Menor's racing operation. I basically sold the people at Budweiser on sponsorship when I didn't even have a nut or bolt of my own."

The sponsorship was a good one.

"It was $15,000 cash, which back then was huge," said Hansen. "Before that, my biggest sponsor was $1,000 from Roger Hansen and Sons Livestock, and I thought that was a real big deal. All I had to do for that sponsorship was run thirteen of the fifteen Thursday nights. It was the biggest sponsorship deal of the time back then in 1985."

Half of the cash came from Anheuser Busch headquarters out of St. Louis, while the other half came from Green Bay beer distributor Dean Distributing. The deal also, as expected, came with an unlimited supply of beer.

"It truly was an endless beer scenario," joked Hansen. "They gave me some Budweiser at the meeting. I told them, 'Boy, this is really rough stuff.' They let me have Bud Light in the cooler instead. Jimmy Dean said they had a Scott Hansen racing shirt on display in their museum as some of the things they'd sponsored at that time. That's pretty cool."

Hansen's sponsorship with Budweiser lasted four years.

As a neophyte on the pavement, Hansen solicited the help of one of the best to get started on the right foot.

"Dick Trickle had the mindset similar to (crew chief) Howie Lettow in that he'd rather have a competitor running well and to not be a hazard on the track," explained Hansen. "When we got the asphalt car, myself, Richie Wauters and Jeff Vandermoss drove to Trickle's shop in Wisconsin Rapids. While Dick and I drank a 12-pack of Pabst, Richie copies all of Dick's setups and such from the tracks out of Dick's notebook. Dick was more than willing to share a lot of his secrets with a new guy like me. That's almost unheard of these days. Dick was a class act top to bottom when it came to that. Everything is under lock and key these days."

Being from Green Bay, Hansen started as an outsider.

"(Dave) Valentyne, JJ (Smith), Lowell (Bennett) and (Terry) Baldry were great racers on the dirt, too," said Hansen. "But they were part of that Fox Valley clique and were the top runners there at that time."

It was another driver from outside of the Fox Valley who would give Hansen some of his stiffest competition through the 1980s.

"Bob Iverson had come down every week for years from Michigan, and he was tough – real tough," said Hansen. "We had a great rivalry, and truth is you won't find a nicer guy than Bobby. We had dog fights every single night. Terry Baldry was a close second. He's a great racer and a nice guy. But you know where nice guys finish in this sport. Terry finished second to us a lot back then."

Baldry would go on to win an unprecedented 12 FRRC championships years later – more than any other driver in FRRC history. The success rate was from one end to the other.

"The big reason for our success was great equipment and great people," said Hansen. "That's why I was successful."

Hansen moved down to Milwaukee in 1990.

"Howie Lettow called me for an interview. They wanted me to race for Baker Motorsports in 1989," said Hansen, who won the ASA rookie-of-the-year title in 1989 in his first full-time year of racing. Hansen ran full time on the ASA series and special events around the country.

"Racing for a living was fabulous. I wouldn't have changed anything," said Hansen. "It starts with people. I surrounded myself with people who would not only work for free on the car, but when it came to partying we'd do that, too."

Over the years, Hansen won some big races such as the Dixieland 250 at Kaukauna, the Rockford Nationals at Rockford Speedway in Illinois, and his first ASA win at the Milwaukee Mile.

"There were so many victories," said Hansen. "In 1995 we won twenty-nine out of sixty-seven races. We'd go to Phoenix and the guys from Goodyear Tire would have pools, and they'd get pissed if they didn't get to pick us in their pools."

"(Car builder) Mike Randerson was huge and a great help to my career, too," said Hansen. "Guys like Mike and Howie (Lettow) were great. Surrounding yourself with key people is what life was all about, and I still try to subscribe to that in life after racing."

In 1997, Hansen got the call to move down south to Charlotte, North Carolina – the hub of NASCAR.

"I was out of a job," said Hansen. "I got into an argument with Jerry (Gunderman, car owner) and it was an argument over a pit stop. I thought I was smarter than the rest of the world. Kenny Schrader and I were both racing at Madison one night. I said to Kenny, 'Whenever you're looking for something to do, keep me in mind.' I got my head back on my shoulders and went back to Gunderman for a year first, which was the best thing I ever did."

Hansen wound up racing a NASCAR truck for Schrader. However, the move down south was far from peaches and cream.

"The truck series for me was a downside to the highlights of my career, to be honest," said Hansen. "The engine program was going through something different. I wasn't accustomed to radial tires at the time. Had I had a Hendrick or Rousch truck, maybe things may have been different. Who knows? I wasn't able to bring any of my own people down. I like Kenny Schrader. He's a great guy and a friend, but back then he didn't spend any money on the truck program. I mean, I had more horsepower with those V 6 engines in ASA then that truck had at the time."

Another thing that didn't sit well with Hansen was the political climate with NASCAR.

"Politics and Scott Hansen don't get along well in that industry," quipped Hansen. "When things don't go well, I want to speak my mind like a Tony Stewart. I really wasn't having any fun down there and a little after a year I was done. The truck thing for me just wasn't very fun."

It was also during his stint with the trucks that Hansen suffered the worst wreck of his racing career at Las Vegas Motor Speedway.

"The right front tire blew and I hit the wall hard going into turn three," said Hansen. "I was knocked out cold for the first time in my life. It was a very hard hit. I never experienced that before."

In 2000, Hansen returned to race for Milwaukee-area car owner Don Fanetti.

"We won our last race at the Milwaukee Mile where I won my first race, so that was sort of a fitting end to the career that had come full circle," said Hansen. "It was time to bow out and try something else for a living."

Hansen, now 61, has owned his own trucking company based in the Milwaukee area since 2004.

"I have no regrets at all," he said. "It was a great ride."

Steve Smits in 1984. (Pete Vercauteren photo)

Steve Smits
Quarter-Mile Dominance

It was really tough for Steve Smits to make it every Thursday night to Wisconsin International Raceway. The De Pere sportsman driver worked for the Green Bay and Western Railroad, and there were simply many Thursday nights Smits would be on a train somewhere, hours away from WIR and couldn't make it.

He worked trades with co-workers for many years, took vacation days and did whatever he could to make it to the track. In a career that began full time in 1984 and wrapped up in 1999, Smits earned four sportsman titles on the tight quarter-mile in 1989 and 1997 thru 1999. What's most impressive about those accomplishments is that he took off of racing from 1991 to 1996.

Although he grew up as a fan watching races at his hometown dirt track in De Pere, the track was closed in 1980, so Smits and his brother, Jerry Smits, began attending races at WIR. It didn't take long before they built a race car.

"I actually ran the last three races of the 1983 season," said Smits. "We built a car that was sort of a sister car for Bob or Jim Duchow. I remember going down the front stretch one of those first few times, and Bryce Spoehr came blasting by me and I thought, 'Boy, I've got a lot to learn,'" said Smits. "I really took a liking to the quarter-mile. We didn't have a lot of money."

Jerry and Steve hung the bodies on their cars and did their own interiors.

"Jerry built all of my motors and we saved money there," said Smits. "I taught myself how to weld. I always wanted to know how and why something worked."

Smits qualified for the feature on opening night in 1984, which was very rare for a rookie driver. With only three races the prior year under his belt, Smits was still considered a rookie.

"I remember starting in row two and I got the lead on lap two and was thinking, 'Well, at least I can say I led the feature,'" recalled Smits. "The race went green-to-checkered, and right before the race ended, I remember looking over and I saw Kurt Johnson coming on fast. (The race) went without a yellow and that pretty much won it for me."

As the years marched on, Smits and his brother took great pride in being competitive and top points finishers despite having to miss nights occasionally because of his work schedule.

"We always seemed to be somewhere between second through fifth in the final points, and a lot of times we had to miss a night because I'd be on the train somewhere," explained Smits.

Smits had fierce rivalries with Rod Wheeler and Rick Spoo.

"One night at WIR, Rod took me out, so I waited two nights later and I took him out at 141 (Speedway)," said Smits. "I regret doing it, but at the time I didn't see it that way."

During his final few years, Smits tangled with Bonduel's Greg Wichman.

"Truth be told, they are good guys and I get along with them," he said. "But back then, it got pretty intense."

Smits decided to hang up his helmet after his final track championship in 1999.

"I was lucky over the years. I never had to restub my race car and never really bent the suspension up much at all," said Smits.

Looking back on the successes he had, Smits actually regrets chasing points titles.

"When you're in the title hunt, you're always watching the point standings and looking to see where everyone else is," said Smits. "I really think those guys who ran the semi-feature and the first and second heats probably had more fun along the way. It wasn't real hard to get caught up in those points battles. If you would take the points out of it, you could probably even run better."

After Smits retired from racing, his brother hooked up with Randy Rahn of Brillion and pitted for him, and later on helped Green Bay's Brett Piontek with his super late model. Jerry Smits is now a technical inspector on Thursday nights at WIR.

Steve Smits still has two racing chassis in his shop. One is an older Lefthander chassis last driven by Eddie Hoffmann for Mike Butz in the mid-1990s. The other is a dirt modified Smits planned on racing at 141 Speedway on the pavement when it was still tar.

"I'm retired, but I guess you could never say never," said Smits when it came to pondering a comeback. "Determination, I feel, was the key to our success. We built most of our own stuff. Now everybody buys their equipment. The cars all look the same these days."

Pete Berken in 1981. (Pete Vercauteren photo)

Pete Berken
Pushing the Envelope

When you think of a driver who pushed the envelope and worked every possible angle of any "gray area" in the rulebook, Pete Berken comes to mind. The sixty-four-year-old from Appleton was loyal to Mopar products for the better part of his racing career at Wisconsin International Raceway. His cars sported eye-catching paint schemes and unique body styles during the heyday of the sportsman class in the early 1980s.

"I was a big Dodge guy when I was young, and I was buddies with Dave Thompson and Rene Grode when they built that Dodge Dart," said Berken. "I got my start hanging around those guys and I pitted for them when they started racing at Apple Creek."

Berken got bitten badly enough by the racing bug that he and a buddy decided to build a car themselves in the early 1970s.

"Mark Heling and I built a car and we were going to take turns driving it," said Berken. "I drove it one night at Apple Creek. I told him after that I just wanted to work on it. He drove it for a year."

In 1974, Berken teamed up with his neighbor, Eddie Kielcheski, wheeling a Dodge Charger on the dirt and asphalt that Berken had purchased from Bob Abitz.

"We took turns driving and we'd run everywhere – Oshkosh, Seymour, Shawano, WIR, and De Pere," said Berken. "When I bought that car from (Bob) Abitz, he gave me all of his Mopar parts – a lot of parts for those 440 engines and stuff."

Berken got some help from a man who would go on to become a national dirt late model fame hall of famer – Pete Parker of Kaukauna.

"I rented a shop and worked out of Pete's shop," said Berken. "He helped me build my first and second cars. They were both number 04. Dave Klink had number 41 at WIR, so I couldn't take that number. There were so many cars and you couldn't have double numbers then. Gary Vercauteren was a Fox River Racing Club officer. He told me that number 40 was taken. Gary suggested we take 04, so we did. Gary picked out our number for us."

Being a true Mopar guy, Berken developed a fan following with those loyal to the Dodge brand.

"I was unique with the Chrysler products," explained Berken. "My car was the first Chrysler product to win on the quarter-mile. Dave (Thompson) owned Appleton Crankshaft and we never went anywhere else to build our motors. They were good to go."

One of the disadvantages in running Mopar power was it could be tougher to get parts.

"We ran the big block motors and we'd still get out-motored," said Berken. "Having Pete Parker helping me, we mixed in some dirt track technology with the asphalt stuff. Some of it was luck and hitting the right thing. We had a pretty dominant car for a few years."

Among Berken's chief rivals with whom he traded paint with regularly were Dennis Dietzen and Jim Duchow.

"I was real good rivals with (Jim) Duchow," recalled Berken. "He was more about horsepower with his program and I was more about handling. My car was fast. I had the track record there for a long time until Rod Wheeler finally broke it. I earned seventeen feature wins and I did it the hard way, starting in the back. I was always in the fast dash, so we were always coming through traffic."

Berken won two or three sportsman titles, depending who you talk to.

Berken's official crowns came in 1980 and 1981. Here's what went down in August 1985 according to Berken:

"I was leading points at the end of the year. On the second to last night of the year, the tech officials were checking stuff and they checked my spindles and they deemed them to be illegal. I was suspended for one week. But the problem was the final points night rained out. So the club took my title away from me. There was some real bad blood for a while.

According to Abitz, who was FRRC's tech inspector at the time, the spindles were indeed not stock and therefore deemed illegal.

"I went to court and sued the Fox River Racing Club to get my track championship back. Basically then, the rulebook said you could do "X, Y or Z" to the spindles, but not "W" like I did. It was a gray area we took advantage of. It was still a stock spindle. We cut the upper part and welded it on. The rulebook didn't say you could or couldn't do it. It was still a stock spindle. We built all our own stuff. We didn't want to buy nothing, so we made our own stuff.

"Outagamie County Circuit Court Judge Luebke agreed with me. In his eyes, I did nothing wrong, but because the club was a club, he could not overrule a club decision. He scolded the officers and told them to 'get their rules better.' And now, the last thing they have in the rules in the FRRC rulebook it states, 'The officers have the right to make the final decision on any of the rules.' I always call that the Pete Berken rule."

In addition to racing at WIR, Berken ran 141 Speedway in Francis Creek and Slinger Super Speedway weekly.

"I had some notes from one of those years and I raced eighty nights in one year," Berken exclaimed. "I remember finishing second, second, and third in points at those three tracks. We only had seven features that we didn't finish that year. It was a pretty good track record and it was either in '83 or '84 we pulled that off."

Berken's last year running the quarter-mile exclusively was 1985.

"I raced late model for Dale Koehler for a few years," said Berken. "We started traveling and doing some other things."

Berken purchased a new Lefthander chassis and ran the entire ARTGO Challenge series, finishing second in the rookie-of-the-year standings to Kevin Cywinski.

"We'd race in Michigan, Illinois, Indiana, and the Milwaukee Mile," he said. "We learned a lot traveling and running ARTGO with guys like (Scott) Hansen, (Ted) Musgrave and (Dick) Trickle. Even Mark Martin would show up and run those once in a while."

Later in the 1980s, Berken would become friends with fellow racer Tom Spierowski. The duo partnered up and raced WIR's half-mile.

"I hung it up for a while in 1990 and came back in 1994," said Berken. "I had begun building up my business, Pete's Auto Repair."

The last season Berken raced super late models was 2008. Even after he hung up his helmet, Berken never missed a Thursday night race dating back to 1976. While he didn't climb behind the wheel himself, in more recent years he mentored a number of younger drivers including Sawyer Effertz, Jesse Oudenhoven and Spierowski's son, TJ Spierowski.

"I really enjoyed working behind the scenes and helping three young kids get into this sport," said Berken.

Duchow, an old rival of Berken's, reached out for some assistance in 2016. Duchow was FRRC club president in 2016.

"They started a new Outlaw late model class on the quarter-mile, and he sort of wanted to use me as a spokesperson for it," said Berken. "They are trying to get this class up and running and shake out some of the older cars laying around. We want to keep this division very affordable. Duchow and I really want to get this class going again on the quarter-mile."

The division was renamed the "WIR quarter-mile limited late model" class and runs a partial schedule on Thursday nights.

Berken, who was the Wisconsin Fans for Auto Racing (WFAR) sportsman of the year recipient in 1980, spends six months living in Appleton and six months in Florida.

Jim Duchow in 1983. (Pete Vercauteren photo)

Jim Duchow
Racing Cop

The seeds of racing passion for many Fox Valley-area racers were planted at the Outagamie County Speedway – otherwise known as Apple Creek, in the mid-1960s. Such was the case for Jim Duchow.

"My dad, LeRoy Duchow, used to take me as a youngster down there when I was nine or ten years old," recalled Duchow, of Appleton. "We'd also go down to Slinger, which was dirt at that time, and Chilton and Plymouth to watch the modifieds. Those cars were really cool."

The young Duchow was so enthralled by the racing scene that he took matters into his own hands one day in 1968.

"I was thirteen years old and it was the first big race at WIR on the half-mile with the paved track," recalled Duchow. "Dad had to work that day and we only had one car. So I rode my ten-speed bike fifteen miles from the north side of Appleton to the track. And County Road CE wasn't even in then! There was no way I was missing that race. AJ Foyt and Jack Bowsher were there, along with Don White. But I remember watching Butch Hartman race and it was just so neat."

During Duchow's high school years from 1969 to 1973, he and his dad frequented the dirt track circuit of half-miles at De Pere, Shawano and Seymour.

"Those tracks were the hotbed of racing locally," Duchow said. "We really didn't even attend WIR weekly yet at that point. Dad wasn't even really that mechanically inclined, but he loved taking me to the races."

Duchow began getting his hands dirty in the early to mid-1970s, pitting for Appleton drivers Gary Sieg and Wayne Weckwerth.

"That's how I started to get a little bit of mechanical knowledge of sorts with race cars," Duchow pointed out. "I remember Wayne built that '66 Chevelle of his on a '57 Chevy frame. He built it behind Baumgart's Tire and Auto in Appleton."

That '66 Chevelle would become Duchow's first race car, as he wheeled it in the sportsman class in a debut in 1977.

"I remember my first race," said Duchow. "Dan Peterman and I started on the front row of the first heat. Dan spun on the start and we had to restart it. I hung on and won that race, my first one ever."

That year the sportsman class began to develop some talent, and it made Duchow and many other younger drivers better within the next few years.

"Around 1980, I was starting to make the feature on a fairly regular basis, which was a tall order," said Duchow. "The feature started fourteen cars, and the qualifying points they paid certainly helped for guys running for points, and to try and eliminate sandbagging, too."

The first feature flags for Duchow came in 1981, and it wasn't long until the track championships started coming his way.

"I was able to win three of them in the '80's," Duchow said. "I remember one year, Kurt Johnson won the track title when I decided to take a year off. I couldn't sit on the sidelines very long and got right back into it."

Among the chief rivals with whom Duchow mixed it up were Pete Berken, Dave Van Elzen, Johnson and Chuck Grall.

"Al Golueke was tough then, too, but Pete Berken was a real rival to me," said Duchow. "But while we raced hard on the track, we were pretty good friends off the track.

"I was always in the fast dash, so that meant I started near the back for every feature. Those features were only twenty laps on that quarter-mile, so to get to the front was a challenge with a fourteen-car field, to say the least. There wasn't racing like it is now, where guys beat and bang. Guys raced clean. There was respect for one another's equipment. You took care of your equipment because you knew you were going to be the one fixing it. There wasn't some dad or uncle who was going to do it for you. You did it yourself. That played into it."

Duchow remembers a violent wreck in 1985 that forced him to take a week's vacation just to repair his battered race car.

"I came back the following Thursday after the crash and won that night," Duchow exclaimed.

Duchow's final year on the quarter-mile was 1985.

"I got together with Tom Rosera in '86," said Duchow. "We moved up to the half-mile to run late model. Tom was my car owner and crew chief. We put together one of his old race cars for the half-mile that year."

Duchow earned rookie of the year honors in 1987.

"I had car number 12, because when I was a police officer for one year in the city of Montello, my badge number was 11. Number 11 was taken when I started racing, so I took number 12," he explained.

Over the years, Duchow would sport different car numbers, including 85, 3 and 66. His first late model feature win on the half-mile came in 1989.

"Guys like JJ (Smith) were in that race, and Scott Hansen and Dave Watson, so it was pretty neat," said Duchow, who earned the division's most improved driver award the previous year.

Despite getting shut out from any feature wins in 1990, Duchow was able to chalk up seven fast time awards that year.

When he wasn't racing, Duchow was a patrolman for the Outagamie County Sheriff's Department. Fortunately, his work hours were never an issue for him.

"I never missed a race because of work," Duchow explained. "I did a lot of trades with guys and that helped me out a ton."

Duchow took the next two years off of racing – sort of.

"In 1992, Todd Tetzlaff was racing and got into a bad crash on the dogleg," said Duchow. "His dad, Monte Tetzlaff, called me and asked me if I'd finish out the remainder of the season in their car, mainly to honor their sponsor commitments. That was around June. At the same time, Tom

(Rosera) and I were building a Mid-American car for the new series Gary Vercauteren was starting up."

Duchow ran the Mid-American Series when it launched in 1993, and for the first time in his career, he ventured to other paved tracks in the Midwest.

"It was a little intimidating at first, especially at tracks like Madison," Duchow explained. "The series was profitable for me. It paid well. One year I made $17,000 in prize and point fund money running that series. I got some fast time bonus money they had. We bought a '78 Olds Cutlass from Zeb's Auto Salvage for $100. We had a real nice, steel-bodied race car we were able to put together for under $8,000. At the time, the cost of late models were getting out of hand. They had sponsorship from Shopko. Gary had a real nice deal going there."

In the Mid-American Series, Duchow would scrap with drivers such as Chicagoland ace Eddie Hoffmann and Roger "The Bear" Regeth.

"Larry Richards was tough from Montello," he said. "Those guys were the top guns."

Duchow returned to weekly Thursday night racing at WIR in 1995. Three seasons later, he would hook up with Denny Lamers of Lamers Motorsports in Appleton, which had fielded midgets on the dirt at Angell Park Speedway in Sun Prairie, Wisconsin.

"Denny wanted to have a stock car racing at Kaukauna," said Duchow. "He decided to get a car out there and got the big sponsorship from Les Stumpf Ford. He was going to pick either myself, Rod Wheeler or Jeff Van Oudenhoven, excluding (Terry) Baldry at the time. It was between us three. Monte (Tetzlaff) worked on Lamers' midgets, so I had an inside track there. I got the call in January of '98, and for the first time in my career I was running somebody else's equipment."

Duchow ran in what was called the limited late model class, which is now referred to as the late model division, for four years. He won the 2008 division crown at WIR and did some traveling with Ron Varney's short-lived ASA tour.

Among the biggest wins of Duchow's career was in 2000 at Rockford (Illinois) Speedway.

"I won the MARS late model series race there during the National Short Track Championships," said Duchow. "The worst wreck I had was at Plover

(Golden Sands Speedway) in '98. I started in the front row of the dash. I got out there late and started the race on cold tires. I flew off the track. I remember the car flying up the embankment, I could see the sky and I rolled and crashed hard into the wall. I was out cold for fourteen minutes. The next thing I remember is waking up with Monte (Tetzlaff) talking to me in an ambulance on the way to the hospital in Stevens Point. That was a rough one."

After hanging up his helmet from full time racing in 2015, Duchow decided to run for Fox River Racing Club president and got the job. Duchow had been the FRRC club secretary in 2000 and 2001, so it was not totally unfamiliar territory for him.

"Back then, it was not so hard to be a club officer and a racer at the same time," said Duchow. "Too many prejudices are there and the officers nowadays have too many things to do. I decided to run because I didn't like the direction the club was headed," said Duchow. "I wanted it to be like it was in the '80s, where at the end of the night guys could say, 'We had fun tonight.' This is supposed to be fun. And that's my goal."

Lowell Bennett in 1981. (Pete Vercauteren photo)

Lowell Bennett
Family Tradition

There's little question Lowell Bennett has the record for most laps on the Wisconsin International Raceway half-mile of any active driver. The second-generation driver from Neenah was introduced to the sport as a youth, and in 2016 celebrated his fortieth year of racing at the age of fifty-seven.

"Dad used to race Shiocton, Leo's Speedway in Oshkosh, and Shawano and De Pere, too," said Bennett of his father, Bobby Bennett. "I remember everything all the way back to the coupe days when it all started."

The first time Bennett attended a race with his dad, known as "Mr. B," was at Outagamie Speedway.

"Dad didn't race that night. He was probably broke," said Bennett. "I was four or five years old. He put me in the grandstand. He told some people to watch me. He bought me a cherry pop and he went in the pits. The bathroom then was an eaves trough. I remember it like yesterday."

"I actually worked on the cars before I got into pits," he said. "Back then, you couldn't go in the pits until you were fourteen. My friend and I in

Greenville were the only ones who could put the header bolts in. The exhaust pipes were so big with the Hemi Dodge. I was probably ten years old and was helping out with Dad's cars."

Tagging along with "Mr. B," Bennett couldn't get enough of the racing fix.

"Growing up with him, I remember sneaking into the pits when I was thirteen when Dad was racing at De Pere," recalled Bennett. "That was the first track I was really able to get into. Back then, women weren't even allowed in the pits. As a kid it was all larger than life to me. De Pere was thriving then. This was the early '70s. Dad had bought that '72 Chevelle from Jerry Smith. Those nights there it was so packed I remember seeing people sitting in the aisles."

That Chevelle the elder Bennett drove was built by Lynn Blanchard, Jerry Smith, and an assist from Mike Randerson. Ironically, Bennett would many years later marry Sue Blanchard, Lynn's daughter.

"Mr. B" never pushed his son into racing.

"For me, it was simply a matter of time until I could afford to go racing," said Bennett. "I worked my tail off as a teenager so I could afford to buy that car from my dad. The only thing my dad bought me was a driver's suit from Wally Jors, ironically just weeks before he died. I bought that Chevelle from my dad for $2,000, and that was without the engine."

The Chevelle was a tank, an older, slower car compared to some of the newer cars that were coming out in the mid-1970s.

"When I bought that car, the bought chassis like the Boyce chassis were coming out," Bennett explained. "My tank of a car weighed close to 3,800 pounds. Those other cars were likely 3,000 pounds."

Bennett won in his debut outing – a heat race at Shawano Speedway.

"I remember vividly passing a guy named Jerry Running for the win," said Bennett. "Corny Schmidt and Jake Hashbarger were in that race, too."

The heavy car was a beast to wrestle.

"I had a Toyota seat from the wrecking yard, and I weighed 165 pounds soaking wet," said Bennett. "When I came in, Kathy Dunn (now Kathy Carpenter) was the trophy gal that night. My car was overheating so I skipped going in victory lane and went straight to the hauler. I was exhausted from a 10-lap heat race. I was laying on the ground tired, and Bob Abitz walks over and says, 'Lowell, you got to get up. People are coming over to see you.'"

Lowell's first taste of WIR came that first year.

"Mike Lemke had got some used tires from Tom Reffner," said Bennett. "He had a rental car and he put them on the roof and tied them on there with a rope. He brought over these tires that were hard as a rock. I liked dirt. I kept the screen in it for a windshield. I went there a couple of times that year."

Despite still being a high school student, Bennett quickly got valuable seat time running whenever and wherever he could. The team ran Leo's in Oshkosh Tuesdays, De Pere Sundays and Shawano Saturdays.

"My first paycheck was $87. I worked for my dad," Bennett said. "I got to use my dad's burned-off tires. Lynn Blanchard helped me out a lot with motors. I'd take Jerry Smith's bent-up wheels, take a torch to them, heat them up and paint them white and reuse them."

During the next couple of seasons, Bennett's racing at WIR became a weekly endeavor. His first feature win came at a dirt track at Luxemburg Speedway in 1977.

"We scored a clean sweep (which meant Bennett nabbed fast time, won his heat, and the feature) and I took home $104," said Bennett. "I remember winning my first feature in Shawano in 1980. I beat Dave Gulmire for the win."

Mike Randerson was a Howe dealer in 1981 and built three cars designed to race both surfaces.

"MJ McBride, myself and Cliff Ebben ran those cars," said Bennett. "MJ ran a little bit, and Cliff and I had more success running both surfaces."

Bennett was the last driver in the state in 1981 to run both surfaces with one race car. He won the Shawano title with ten victories, the rookie of the year title at Slinger, and was fourth in points at WIR. One weekend, Bennett won at Shawano on Saturday and also ran an ARTGO race at WIR the following afternoon.

"I won a semi during the ARTGO show," Bennett said. "I won at Slinger the second time I ever ran there that same day. I was drained driving home from Slinger Sunday night."

After the 1981 season, Bennett and his crew grew tired of the time-consuming endeavor of switching the car over from dirt to asphalt each week. Another incident during the off season before the 1982 season was pretty much the icing on the cake for Bennett and his dirt track days.

"Shawano Speedway had a secret drivers meeting and they changed the rules for their late models, including motors," said Bennett. "Back then, MJ McBride had a lot of say and pull in what went on over there. So we ran a couple of races early in the year in '82 on dirt, and that was the end of me running at Shawano."

Bennett continued to pay his dues at WIR and was content to even make the feature every Thursday night.

"I didn't win my first feature at WIR until 1985," said Bennett. "The field was stacked for the weekly show. We had a lot of tough customers. Rich Somers was still running there. It was tough to make a feature most nights. Back in the day, nobody tired-up (putting four new tires on to race the feature) every night. That all changed when Steve Marler got involved with Scott Hansen's program, and they'd put new tires on all the way around for the features."

Bennett also began running full time at Slinger Speedway north of Milwaukee.

"We'd even run some ARTGO shows when we had the time and the money," said Bennett. "I think the fact I raced multiple times a week, and I continue to be a two-night-a-week racer, helped me over the years on Thursday nights."

Bennett was on a roll in the early 2000s. If he wasn't winning at WIR, he was winning at Slinger. He was almost always a top-five car every night.

"Things were going well at that point, so well that around 2001 I was actually making money racing," he said. "We were fortunate enough to have some really good sponsors come on board. We didn't wreck, we won races and were ahead of the game."

Bennett said he had $20,000 "laying around," so he decided to take the financial plunge and purchase a car to run a limited schedule in NASCAR's Busch Series.

"We bought a Busch car in March of 2002," said Bennett." We bought the hauler I have yet today. It was either pay the IRS the money we had been making or do something else with it. So we bought a Busch car. I got ahold of Joe Shear Jr. He came up and helped us finish the car. The first race was at Milwaukee. Wegner Automotive helped me out with a motor on it. The following race was IRP (Indianapolis Raceway Park) in Indianapolis."

Bennett made every Busch show he qualified for. Still, he was in way over his head.

"We were at a drivers meeting in Memphis and Kenny Wallace yells, 'Hey Bennett, how'd you do when you tested here?' I said, 'Tested? Heck, I've never even seen this place!' He was a hoot. It was a lot of fun running those NASCAR races and I wouldn't trade it for anything. But it was very, very expensive. I ran on my own dime.

"We put all the tires on the credit card. The tire bill to run one weekend was $14,000. It was $25,000 to rent a motor for a normal guy. I had to hire a crew chief. We'd hire a truck crew or a Cup crew – whoever was there for that weekend. For a little guy going down there, it was tough. We were so close in 2002 at the end of the season to getting a big sponsor to do Busch. We had two professional people in North Carolina working on sponsors. This was after 9/11 and the economy started to tighten up. So we didn't get anything."

The final NASCAR race Bennett ran was in 2004 at Richmond International Raceway.

"We had a top-ten car there and one of (Rick) Hendrick's guys t-boned me," Bennett said. "The following year, NASCAR made a lot of rules changes. We'd buy used Cup tires for $250 apiece used instead of $450 apiece. When NASCAR did away with all of that, we for sure couldn't afford it anymore. So we wound up selling the Busch car."

As of 2016, Bennett has won five Thursday night WIR super late model titles, including five Red, White and Blue crowns. He's also won seven Slinger Nationals titles. Bennett added another impressive series win to his resume in 1997, capturing the World Series of Asphalt racing championship at New Symrna Speedway in Florida.

The next generation of Bennett racers is already on the track. Bennett describes his son, Braison Bennett, as a carbon copy of himself.

"He's got the genes on both sides of the family," said Lowell Bennett. "He got to be ten years old and he wanted to race something. One night, he and I went to the drag races at WIR. He thought they were real cool. I told him I didn't have a lot of time to devote to that. So he went to his mom. She said, 'Sure, bring home straight A's and we can do it.' So I went down and bought him a dragster."

Bennett quickly discovered that the drag racing world and the oval track world at WIR were two completely different worlds.

"I knew absolutely nothing about drag racing – nothing," said Bennett. "The drag racing people, many of them knew who I was, but most of them really didn't have any genuine interest where we were making left hand turns and going in circles. Now some of these drag racing folks come to the oval track on Thursday nights to watch me compete."

Braison Bennett raced drags through his teen years and quickly climbed his way through the short track food chain.

"He started out in a four-cylinder and later would move up to the late model class," said Lowell Bennett. "He's got talent, but there's no free ride here. My dad never gave me one and he's also got to earn everything he gets. He pays for his program all on his own."

Braison Bennett was the 2016 WIR late model track champion and also the Red, White and Blue champion.

"There are some parents that push their kids in this sport, and that's something I won't do," said Lowell Bennett. "You've got to keep it fun. Keep (your kids) in a class that they are totally comfortable in. Let them have their fun before they move on up."

Bennett's daughters, Season and Jurnee, also drag race at WIR and Lowell Bennett shows no signs whatsoever of slowing down.

"I see myself doing this at least ten more years," he said. "On Thursday nights at WIR, I'm the old guy. But down at Slinger, you've got Conrad Morgan, Jerry Eckhardt and Fred Winn who are all older than me yet, so I've got a ways to go."

Gordie Sannes at a Sunday Special in 1983. (Pete Vercauteren photo)

Gordie Sannes
Loyalty

The birth of Patty Sannes in 1963 is what launched the racing career for the Sannes Brothers.

"Patty was born and Mom wanted us all out of the house, so Dad took us to Luxemburg to the races to watch," said Gordie Sannes. "That was all it took. We were all hooked after that."

The Sanneses had a second cousin from Tilleda (Shawano County), Wisconsin, named Bobby Maas, who raced at Shawano Speedway on Saturday nights.

"We started going to the races at Shawano to watch him, too," said Lee Sannes. "We never missed a night."

Gordie couldn't stand to be a spectator for long. A student at Green Bay West, he and his buddy, Bob Nowack, got ahold of an old race car.

"Gary Hammond had an old purple car that had been sitting behind this barn for years," recalled Gordie. "We took it, fixed it up and went racing with it."

The car made its debut at Luxemburg Speedway in 1971 with Nowack at the wheel.

"Bob raced it once and then he went into the Air Force," said Gordie. "I took over racing after that."

Gordie's first race was 1971 in Shiocton. It was a small, banked race track.

"We'd argue for 25 cents a point back then," said Gordie. "Pappy Diemel was fast there. Cork Surprise ran there along with Roger Paul and Denny Teschke."

It would wind up being a very long night for the Sannes Bros.

"We towed that car from Green Bay's west side along Highway 54 to Shiocton with a tow bar behind a '64 Buick LeSabre four-door," said Larry Sannes. "We bent the tie rod that night. We weren't smart enough to know how to fix it. After the races were done, we crawled along the shoulder of Highway 54 at 20 miles an hour all the way back home to Green Bay. That tire was just squealing."

During the next few years, Lee and Larry also took their turns behind the wheel.

"We were all pretty green," admitted Lee. "It took us eight races one year to figure out we had a bad coil. We didn't know much at all about cars. We all went to tech school then and got smart, I guess."

Lee Sannes ran the sportsman class at Wisconsin International Raceway in 1974 and 1975.

"Back then they had a rule that you had to buy your tires used from a late model team, and we bought ours from Larry Schuler," said Lee. "Paul Jochman was really fast back then. I remember that."

While Lee ran the quarter-mile, Gordie ran a '65 Mustang on both the local dirt tracks and on WIR's half-mile.

"After a while, Lee quit racing, and when Gordie went full time late model, we started putting all of our time and effort into one car," said Larry Sannes.

The first "real" tricked-up race car Gordie had was in 1976, when they purchased a Boyce Trackburner chassis through Mike Schmelzer at Bay Speed Center, which was the hot ticket in the '70s.

"That was a state-of-the-art chassis back then," said Lee. "The car had a '72 Nova body on the frame."

Gordie ran the car on dirt and on asphalt at WIR. 1977 saw the team go to asphalt full time.

"On dirt, some of those guys would come in with three or four sets of dirt tires because there was no real tire rule on dirt," said Gordie. "I remember Pete Parker showing up with a huge supply of tires at De Pere, and I wasn't real good at reading a dirt track and how it was changing anyways. Plus, we were cleaning a ton of clay off the car. That got old. We didn't have a fancy pressure washer back then either. It was just time for a change."

The Sannes Bros. were among the last of the late model teams who ran big block, 427-cubic-inch engines.

"Guys were getting rid of their big beefy motors over the years, so we were able to get the parts for those big blocks real, real cheap," explained Larry Sannes.

Gordie had a reputation as a clean driver, and he was almost always a top-ten points finisher. As a result of his sportsmanship, he was awarded the Jim Pagel Sportsmanship Award in addition to the Can Do Award.

"I asked (Fox River Racing Club officer) Judi Monday why I got the award," said Gordie. "She said after Jim Duchow passed us on the last lap to win the feature after we led the whole way, I got out of my car and shook his hand. I guess nobody does that anymore."

The half-mile at WIR has been known to claim some horrific wrecks over the years. Gordie was not immune to that.

"One year, I flipped and took out seven fence posts along the backstretch fence," said Gordie. "I remember hitting every one of those posts. That one was bad. I remember my helmet hitting inside the roof of my car. Tom Spierowski came up and got into us and we went for a ride."

The Sannes Bros. car became a "track mule" of sorts for John McKarns and his ARTGO series on a few occasions.

"We had (NASCAR stars) Steve Park in our car and Harry Gant one time," said Gordie. "Very nice guys. Harry was more content talking about his farm than anything else."

But it was an ARTGO race in the mid-1990s when a very young Tony Stewart drove the Sannes Bros. entry one weekend.

"We were down at Illiana (Indiana) Speedway and we showed up before Tony did," said Larry Sannes. "He walks up to us with his pilot, his girlfriend, and some young kid he was mentoring and says, 'Are you guys here to make laps or are you guys here to try and win?' He was a pretty serious racer."

Stewart used his pull to thwart off the tech inspectors.

"I remember Clem (Droste, ARTGO official) was giving us a hard time because our spoiler was mounted a bit forward," said Gordie Sannes. "Tony said, 'I'll take care of this.' He went and talked to Clem and after that we never had a problem the rest of the night."

That Illiana ARTGO race marked a milestone of sorts. It was the first time Stewart had raced against Matt Kenseth.

"We were pitted next to Mike (Butz, Kenseth's car owner), so that's pretty significant," said Gordie. "Tony was working on our car like it was his own. He got right into it."

Stewart raced for the Sanneses three nights later at WIR in the Dixieland race. Gordie did not race because he had a prior commitment with his sons with a Boy Scout outing.

"John (McKarns) had Tony staying in some hotel in Chilton. I called John and told him we'd arranged to pick Tony up from the airport in Green Bay instead," said Larry Sannes. "I got him a room at the Radisson Hotel across the street by the casino."

Stewart stayed up the better part of the night gambling in the casino and showed up the next day at WIR just in the nick of time for a media obligation.

"When Stewart got done with a news conference Monday one night before the Dixieland, the skies began to darken and he said, 'I've got to get some hot laps in,' and Tony got some practice in before the weather got bad." said Larry Sannes.

"During that practice session, Kenseth, who was a track champion at WIR, told Stewart, 'Follow me, I'll show you the fast way around this track.' That lasted about five laps," said Larry. "Tony started running his own line and was fast. He made it work.

"After that practice session, we sat at our shop and just talked racing. We asked him if he wanted to go eat at some restaurant. He told us, 'I've been on the road for almost thirty days straight at Indianapolis, testing cars for John Menard when I'm not running my own car. I'd love nothing better than a home-cooked meal.'"

So an impromptu cookout with steaks on the grill took place at the Sannes homestead. Many people found out through word of mouth that Tony

Stewart was in town and they had many curious fans show up at their shop, where Tony was enjoying a grilled steak with all the fixings. Stewart wound up finishing mid-pack in that event.

"If we wouldn't have had a tire go down, I think we would have had a chance to win that thing," said Lee.

Afterward, Stewart sent a letter to the Sannes team, thanking them for the opportunity to drive their race car in the ARTGO events.

The final year Sannes Bros. fielded a team was in 2003, when they ran the MARS touring series.

"The last hurrah for us was Sauk Centre Speedway (I- 94) Speedway at a MARS race, "said Gordie. "We were third in points. I ended up crashing out hard there. I broke some ribs and ended up in the hospital. That was it for me after that. The car was junk. We busted the transmission, the rear end and even the motor."

The Sanneses still have a number of family members involved in racing. Gordie's sons, Neil and Evan Sannes, still compete on Thursday nights. Gordie has two new nephews who race as well, Brett Van Horn and Chad Butz.

And as for Patty Sannes? She wound up marrying Mike Butz, championship car owner at WIR.

Terry Baldry in 1984. (Pete Vercauteren photo.)

Terry Baldry
Smooth as Silk

Track announcers would often cringe when Terry Baldry would wind up in victory lane. It wasn't because Baldry was a bad guy. On the contrary.

The problem with Baldry was two-fold. For one, he was a man of very few words. During pre- and post-race interviews, track announcers quickly discovered getting Baldry to provide anything beyond one- or two-word answers was akin to a painful visit to the dentist. Baldry did his talking behind the wheel of his race car at speed.

The Omro driver also won frequently. Baldry, now sixty-three years old, won an unprecedented twelve super late model titles on Wisconsin International Raceway's half-mile. His feat included six straight championships from 1999 through 2004. Baldry's first crown came in 1982 and his final track championship was in 2010. No other driver in Kaukauna history has even come close to putting up those types of championship numbers.

A man whose reputation was that of a clean driver – not one to rub fenders often – Baldry would just as soon go around a driver than try and squeeze inside of him or through him.

"We started running WIR full time on the pavement in 1979," recalled

Terry Baldry in 1980 (Pete Vercauteren photo)

Baldry. "We were still running some dirt stuff then with the same car at Shawano and De Pere. Leo's Speedway had closed the year before in Oshkosh."

Baldry went full time the following season and raced exclusively at WIR after the track in De Pere shut down.

Baldry's brother, Dennis, served as his crew chief in the early 1980s. The car was owned by their parents, Wallace and Lorraine Baldry.

"That 9:1 compression rule really helped keep the asphalt late model going," explained Baldry. "Before that came around, guys were blowing a lot of motors at Kaukauna. These were lasting us a lot longer, it seemed."

Baldry's first title in 1982 came against some tough customers on Thursday nights.

"I remember Ted Musgrave running there weekly along with Jim Sauter and JJ Smith," said Baldry. "Dave Watson was there, too, and always seemed to have real good equipment."

A few years later, Green Bay's Scott Hansen would come onto the scene and Baldry won his last title in the '80s in 1984. With a trio of track titles under his belt, Baldry began to spread his wings a bit, running the full American Speed Association (ASA) series in 1992. He wound up second in the final rookie of the year standings to Tim Fedewa.

"(Traveling) was okay, but it got to be a grind after a while," said Baldry. "I drove for a guy from Cleveland, Ohio, named Jack Sinclair. They kept the car out in Ohio. That was the first time I was a hired gun. It was a lot cheaper going that route."

The following season, Baldry and his brother chipped in and co-owned the car, and Baldry returned to his winning ways by capturing the 1993 track championship. In 1997, Baldry teamed up with Mike Butz, who was hot off winning a pair of titles with Matt Kenseth in '94 and '95. It didn't take long for those two to mesh as Baldry went on to win the 1997 title.

"I remember we had All Car Automotive Centers (as a sponsor) that year, and we even won Oktoberfest at La Crosse, too," Baldry pointed out. The Oktoberfest win was the last ever under the ARTGO banner, as the series became the NASCAR Re/Max Challenge Series the following year.

The Butz/Baldry combination proved to be tough – very tough.

"The only year I didn't win the title driving for Butz was in 1998, when I broke a vertebrae in my back in a crash at the Dells," said Baldry. "I was out for six weeks. Other than that until that point, we won pretty much everything."

The hired gun from Omro switched over to the De Pere-based BUCO racing team in 2003. New car owner – same result. Baldry won back-to-back titles driving their number 00 car in 2003 and 2004.

"There were different personalities between Butz and BUCO, but they had the same goal in mind as Butz did, and that was to win races and titles," said Baldry. "Every car owner I had was a little bit different."

"He was so damned smooth that guy," said BUCO Racing car owner Mark Patton. "He never got fluttered or fired up. He's real quiet and was always very calm when talking to him on the radio."

One night with using just two new tires underneath their car, Baldry broke the track record with a 19.236, a record that had been held by the late Joe Shear.

"So with just two new tires under the car, Terry crawls out and says to us, 'I left some on the track. I could have probably gone even faster that lap.' He was just incredible," said Patton.

It would be six seasons later before Baldry would reunite with Butz and win his twelfth WIR track championship in 2010. Baldry has raced sparingly since then, with his last time behind the wheel for Butz in 2014 at Kaukauna.

"Terry Baldry had the utmost respect for the equipment he was driving – bar none," said Bob Schafer of Oshkosh. Schafer is a "superfan" who attends over 300 short track races a year. Schafer hasn't missed many races at WIR in his adult life. "Terry's approach was always to find a way to get the car in victory lane and bring it home in one piece. And he almost always did that. It did not matter whose car he was driving. He was always a threat and his moves, especially toward the end of his career, were quite calculated. He's one of the best to ever run WIR."

Retired now as a full time employee from Mercury Marine since 2008, Baldry spends much of his time in the winter months in Nevada. He has plenty of family members who still race, and he attends their races on both dirt and asphalt.

Baldry's son, Brady, has an asphalt super late model he races on occasion, and son Kevin races an IMCA modified on dirt. Grandson Wyatt Blashe races in the T.U.N.D.R.A. super late model series. His daughter, Sarah Blashe, used to race street stocks at WIR, while his son-in-law, Brandon Blashe, a former Fox River Racing Club president, used to race an IMCA stock car on dirt.

Matt Kenseth (center) with car owners Patty and Mike Butz in 1995. (www.danlewisphoto.net)

Matt Kenseth/Patty & Mike Butz
A Star is Born

It was June, 1981. Mike Butz had just graduated from Bay Port High School – a suburban school just north of Green Bay. Butz was sitting in the stands with Debbie Roffers on a Thursday night at Wisconsin International Raceway.

"We were watching Debbie's husband, Wayne, race," recalled Butz, who was still very green behind the ears when it came to anything racing-related. "My brother, Roger Butz, used to work for Gordie Sannes' wife. Gordie was pulling in the pits with his race car and hauler one night and my buddy started pitting for Gordie. I began tagging along and helping them in the pits, too."

That's how Mike met his future wife, Patty Sannes. They would marry in 1986.

"The year I got married I built a sportsman car for my brother, Roger, and things just sort of took off from there as a car owner," he said.

Butz, who would end up co-owning the race cars with his wife, decided to bump up to the half-mile the following season. The team's first "hired gun" was a Milwaukee-area driver named Thom Laimon of Hales Corners.

"Gordie and Larry (Sannes) were friends with Thom, so that's how we got to know him," explained Butz. "We just sort of branched out. Roger never raced a full year on the quarter-mile." That car sported the number 3 and Laimon drove for the Butzes until 1991.

Butz kept his mouth shut and his ears open while traveling at times with Gordie Sannes on the ARTGO circuit, which featured races at asphalt tracks in several Midwestern states.

"I learned so much by traveling with those guys and ARTGO for those years," said Butz. "I'd go back to the hotel room at night when we were at overnight shows and I'd write stuff into a notebook for later reference."

One of the drivers Butz met through the ARTGO circuit and Appleton engine builder Bruce Mueller was West Salem driver Tom Carlson. Tom and his brother, Steve Carlson, were top drivers in western Wisconsin and the ARTGO circuit.

"I struck a deal with Tom Carlson as he'd race for us on Thursday nights at WIR," explained Mike Butz. "In turn, we'd help him out on his pit crew for the ARTGO shows."

"We ended up second in points and won our first feature with Tom," said Patty Butz.

A miscommunication in times well before cell phones thwarted what could have been a WIR track title.

"It looked like rain one night and we couldn't get a hold of him on the landline," said Mike Butz. "He didn't show up that night. Also, we had blown up a motor that Tuesday night during a special and I suspect he didn't think I'd get a replacement motor in. But we did."

As it turned out, the Butzes were all revved up with that night no place to go.

In 1992, New Franken's Kevin Servais was the team's hired gun.

"We wanted a local driver and we got together with Kevin, who Mike actually met during the winter earlier by going to Lefthander to buy a car," said Patty Butz.

While at Lefthander, Mike Butz met a little "cornball of a kid," as Patty Butz described him, who was working the parts counter at Lefthander named Matt Kenseth.

"Ask Wayne Lensing (Lefthander owner) and he was probably sleeping in those racing seats when he wasn't taking inventory of them," Patty Butz joked. "(Kenseth) had asked Mike if he could drive his car up here on Thursday nights. Mike said, 'I can't. I've already got a driver in Kevin Servais.'"

The first time Patty Butz met Kenseth, the young driver projected the furthest image from the clean-cut, NASCAR polish he shows on television.

"When I first met Matt, we stopped at Bruce Mueller's and he was there with Joe Wood," said Patty Butz. "He had a Metallica shirt and some ripped-up jogging pants. He was still pretty much a kid."

Kenseth and Butz officially teamed up the following year in 1993. While Kenseth was already a hotshot as a teenager, he struggled initially when it came to getting around the tricky WIR oval.

"Every week the nose would be taken off the car or so it seemed," said Mike Butz. "He'd tear the car up and he'd pull into our pit and just say, 'Sorry, Uncle Mike.'"

Kenseth won a couple of features that first year, and when he started winning more features and the first of two straight track titles in 1994 and 1995, he became sort of a "heel" as in pro wrestling.

"No one liked him on Thursday nights because he was an outsider," said Patty Butz. "He didn't have an Appleton or a Fox Valley phone number. Some fans would get a Hot Shot racing card from him and they'd rip it up in his face. A lot of those are the same hypocrites who wear Matt Kenseth gear now that he's won in NASCAR. The drivers didn't like him either. He learned the 'slide for life' move from Joe Shear, and he wasn't afraid to mix it up with the other drivers."

"I remember one night he kept his window net up with his helmet on because there were about fifteen people who ran over to the car and they all wanted a piece of him," said Mike Butz. "It was sort of funny because Gene Wheeler had spent a lot of money on Rod (Wheeler's) car, so he thought I was just some country boy who had no business running up there near the front as a car owner. We were always getting into it with the Wheelers it seemed."

One night, Patty Butz had to step in between her husband and Gene Wheeler. However, it was Patty who ended up accidentally getting clocked by Mike as the two car owners were ready to throw dukes.

It didn't take Mike and Patty Butz long to realize Kenseth was headed to bigger and better things – and quickly.

"We knew he was already talking to different people about getting something going down south, and he was also running a car those years for Fred Neilsen, too," said Mike Butz. "There were times he'd get up to WIR late for qualifying and I'd just have Jeff Van Oudenhoven shake the car down for me and get the temperatures up. Then he'd pop in, and go out and set fast time. Matt was a quick thinker. He'd react quickly. You'd try lipping off to him and he'd have a comeback immediately. He was really good at giving feedback."

"Pretty much anybody I ran against up there was a rival to me back then," recalled Kenseth. "I really felt like they viewed me as an outsider. And with the Fox River Racing club running the weekly deal there at Kaukauna, they didn't like outsiders. I was from Madison. I got screwed over on a call one night. I don't even remember the name of the club president at the time, but as far as I'm concerned that club still owes me two hundred dollars.

"I'll never forget I caught the leader on the last lap during a feature. I went to pass him on the outside and took him for the win. He slid up into me and ran into my door and spun himself out. They disqualified me for winning that race. To this day I feel that is the biggest injustice I've ever faced in my racing career. I've always felt when I ran at WIR, the deck was always stacked against me for some reason. Lowell Bennett was a great guy and a real clean racer to run against. Rod Wheeler – he was a good guy, but we always had some battles and some pretty major disagreements with him.

"Kaukauna is a really unique track. It's unlike any other half-mile I'd ever raced before. (Turns) 1 and 2 are a lot different than 3 and 4. It took me awhile to get good there. There is a lot of character there at that place that you can use to your advantage, no doubt."

"Mike and Patty (Butz) were great to me. We had a lot of fun together for a lot of years," Kenseth continued. "We had a blast. It was a lot more fun than things really are now. I mean, we took things seriously, but we also had a lot of fun along the way. We won a ton of races together."

Among Kenseth's most memorable moments was a last-minute decision to run a special at WIR.

"I remember Mike called me up and asked if I wanted to run a Red White and Blue race one Saturday night. We had no intentions of going, so this really was a last-minute deal," said Kenseth. "We got there at the last second. No practice, barely had time to qualify. I was leading the deal with twenty-five laps to go. We never even had time to bleed the brakes. I held up the field and then I got spun and went spinning backwards on the backstretch. For some reason that race stands out among the other ones."

Kenseth headed south in 1996 to run a regional short track series and get one step closer to racing in NASCAR. That year, Eddie Hoffmann, a stud racer from Chicagoland, started out the year for the Butzes.

"Some of the locals didn't like the fact we had Hoffmann run our car, and he was aggressive and a front runner," said Patty Butz. "Some local car owners we raced against called and complained to our sponsor, All Car Automotive, and whined that Hoffmann wasn't a good fit for them and a bunch of other nonsense."

The Butzes felt pressure to remove Hoffmann, and Kenseth came back to wheel the car on occasion at WIR in 1996. From there, a myriad of drivers wheeled cars for the Butzes over the years. In 1997, Butz got together with Terry Baldry, the winningest driver in Fox River Racing Club history, and they won five titles together.

"The guy was smooth as silk," said Mike Butz. "Terry has a lot of respect for other drivers. He had one bad night in the opener in '97 when he got together with somebody else and rolled. Terry walks into the pits and hands me the rear view mirror. He said, 'This is about all that's left of the car.'"

Baldry came back the next week and won the feature.

In addition to Kenseth and Baldry, Van Oudenhoven raced for the Butzes and the duo won four MARS late model series titles together.

"We won at the Milwaukee Mile with Jeff and at I-70 Speedway in Missouri, too," Mike Butz said. "We had some good years with Jeff. He's a good guy and a great racer. I consider him a friend."

In total, the Butzes had more than two dozen drivers wheel their equipment over the years, including a well-funded ace with a promising future from

Minnesota named Andy Hanson in 2007 and 2008.

"His dad's trucking company was a big sponsor, and we had some cars lined up from Rousch Racing to go do this racing thing down south," said Mike Butz. "After the stock market crashed in 2008, his trucking company went belly up like many others and that was the end of that."

The list of drivers who raced for Mike and Patty Butz over the years includes Roger Butz, Thom Laimon, Tom Carlson, Kevin Servais, Matt Kenseth, Eddie Hoffmann, Curt Wausch, Danny Gracyalny, Joe Wood, Terry Baldry, Jason Schuler, Lowell Bennett, Gordie Sannes, Brad Mueller, Doug Mahlik, Jeff Van Oudenhoven, Ryan Mathews, Andy Monday, Neil Knoblock, Josh Bauer, Andy Hanson, Kyle Calmes, Adam White, Dalton Zehr, Jacob Goede, Boris Jurkovic, Ty Majeski, and Chad Butz.

Mike and Patty Butz's son, Chad Butz, a student at Bay Port High School in Howard, wheels his race car now. He was the super late model rookie of the year at Norway (Michigan) Speedway in 2015, and as of this writing had started to branch out and run other tracks, including a practice session at WIR.

The game has changed in super late model racing since 1995. The expenses teams must shell out to put cars on the track have far outpaced the prize money drivers race for.

"The biggest thing is motors. They are really expensive now," said Mike Butz. "Sponsors are hard to find. Some of the bigger ones I've had over the years were $25,000 or $30,000, but you can't find those ones anymore. It's the racers' own fault. They keep voting all these rules in with this new technology and the costs keep going up and up. It's tough. It's a domino effect. If we want to keep racing going in Wisconsin, you've got to control costs."

Retired sportswriter Tom Goff (Joe Verdegan photo)

Tom Goff
Making Deadline

Most short tracks in the United States would be thrilled to have an old school "beat writer" covering their weekly racing activities. Normally, the beat writers for daily newspaper cover traditional "stick and ball" sports. Wisconsin International Raceway was lucky to have Tom Goff around for a long time.

Goff, a native of Greenfield, covered the events at WIR for the *Appleton Post-Crescent* from 1985 up until he retired from writing for the daily newspaper in 2011. Goff continued to act as the track's and Fox River Racing Club's public relations director for two seasons after his retirement.

Goff caught the racing bug when his father would take him to races at the Milwaukee Mile as a youngster.

"Back in the day at the Milwaukee Mile, racing was a real big deal," said Goff. "There were always two USAC stock car races and a champ car race during the Fair week. My dad got us free tickets. My hero was Don White of Keokuk, Iowa. Those were beautiful race cars back then."

Goff actually began as a reporter for the *Kaukauna Times* starting in 1971.

"They hired me sight unseen for a hundred bucks a week," said Goff, who would work for the *Times* for seven years. "Terry McGlone was my news guy. We'd go out there to cover the major events that were there like the Red White and Blue races. He didn't like the weekly, Thursday night races they had at the time. He called those the 'Thursday night crash and bangs.'"

As the years marched on into the 1970s, the *Kaukauna Times* would print most of the stuff sent by track P.R. man Gary Vercauteren.

"I shared the same booth at WIR with Gary for more than twenty years," said Goff. "You didn't find many P.R. guys like Gary. He was real really good. He lived and breathed racing."

Goff got a job at the *Post-Crescent* full time in 1979.

"When Dan Flannery became sports editor there in 1985, he said we needed to have a presence at the track all the time," said Goff. "He'd see the stories sent out and there may be a disqualification or something. Dan felt our readers deserved to know what was going on, so we did a little bit of digging when it came to those sort of things."

As a result, Goff covered all the races at WIR. It helped that Goff lived in Kaukauna, less than five minutes from the track, and for most of his career there the *Post-Crescent* was an afternoon paper.

"I was able to stick around sometimes in the tech area if there was something going on later after the races," Goff pointed out. "So my deadline wasn't an issue, at least not until they became a morning paper later on."

Of all the drivers who always seemed to have interesting quotes for Goff, Minnesota's Jim Weber took the cake.

"Weber was always pushing the limits it seemed, and was always good for a colorful quote or two over the years," joked Goff.

A typical deadline for Goff when the paper went to a morning edition was either 11 p.m. or 11:30 p.m.

"We had these scrolling-type computers with phone couplers that would scroll the story through kind of like a fax," said Goff, describing the limited technology prior to the Internet age. "I would either write from the track or I would just go home and write my story. There were a few times I'd have problems submitting my story and I'd have to drive down to Appleton before the deadline, but that didn't happen very often."

Eventually, WIR acquired email capabilities and Goff was able to simply email his story from the track.

In addition to covering the weekly racing events, Goff would also write a weekly column covering the WIR beat in addition to feature stories on drivers. Among the biggest events he ever covered at WIR was the untimely death of Jim Pagel in 1997.

"I was interviewing Andy Geiger in the pit area when Pagel crashed," said Goff. "Andy was the defending champion the year before in the truck division. We heard the crash and we looked over and saw Pagel's car up against the wall. At first nobody really thought it was a big deal. Cars crashed all the time."

But this crash was different.

"As I was interviewing Andy, it got real quiet and I noticed the track safety crew had put up a black tarp along the spectator fence," Goff recalled. "I told Andy, 'I've got to go see what's going on there,' so I made my way over to turn one where the crash was."

When the local fire department and paramedics arrived on the scene, Goff recognized a familiar face.

"I knew Scott Roebuck, who was one of the paramedics I played softball with, and I asked him what was going on. He simply said, 'I can't talk, we've got a guy fighting for his life,'" said Goff. "I knew then it was bad. And it was a bad deal as he died later on at Theda Clark Hospital in Neenah. I interviewed Jim Pagel many times. He was a great guy – one of the most likeable drivers ever at that track. He had come off a pretty good season. He got the Budweiser ride that year, and unfortunately it was cut short by that tragedy."

Joe Verdegan

Goff got to rub elbows and interview many of the NASCAR drivers when they came to town for the ARTGO Dixieland shows.

"I remember hopping into a van with Dale Earnhardt and Rusty Wallace from the pits, and Dave Valentyne gave us a ride up top. Those guys were pretty cool," said Goff. "They were poking fun of the locals a little bit, but it was good-natured, really. They were decent guys and you could tell they enjoyed doing those appearances."

Goff got to interview Matt "The Brat" Kenseth frequently on Thursday nights before Kenseth hit the big-time in NASCAR.

"I remember writing a column about Matt that basically said, 'This kid won't stick around here long,'" said Goff. "The thing I remember about Matt was he was brash. And he passed cars on the outside most of the time, which was tough to do. I think we all knew he wasn't going to be racing at WIR weekly for too long."

Meeting copy deadlines are a thing of the past for Goff these days, although he still frequents WIR as a fan in the stands.

"I pay my ten bucks and I'll usually sit in the stands with family and enjoy the races," said Goff. "I still am a fan of the races."

Jim Pagel (left) talks over racing strategy with crew member Neil Maas in 1996. (Judi Monday photo)

Jim Pagel
Gone Way Too Soon

Dennis Monday was the last person to speak to Jim Pagel before his untimely death at Wisconsin International Raceway on May 2, 1997. Pagel lost control of his late model stock car during a qualifying lap on the half-mile. His car spun out, spinning clockwise and slamming into the turn one retaining wall flush. Pagel died at Theda Clark Medical Center in Neenah later that night as the result of massive head and chest injuries.

A former racer himself, Monday was Pagel's best friend and a crew member for the Appleton driver in his late model operation, which was owned by Green Bay's Ken Des Jardin.

"I was Jim's spotter the day of that crash," recalled Monday. "Jim had a little trouble with his qualifying efforts. So right before he went out, I'd talk to him a little bit and that day I told him, 'Good luck,' and 'You can do it.' I never said anything to him while he was under green. When the crash happened, I kept asking him if he was okay, and obviously got no response. That race car was a brand new Coleman race car. After the crash we took the car up to Roger's (Van Daalwyk) shed and went over the whole car. We couldn't find anything wrong with the car's suspension. Nothing was out of the ordinary.

"Later that year, about mid-season, we ended up pulling some parts out of the car Jim crashed in and put them into his show car. (Pagel had Budweiser among his many sponsors and used to show the race car off frequently). To fulfill our sponsor obligations, we put Neil (Maas) in the car and went with number 21. We probably didn't get it back out until mid-July or so. We had Lamers Motorsports for a sponsor that year, too.

"Pagel worked as a union carpenter when he passed away. He was engaged to Pam Case. Pagel was a gentleman's gentleman. Everybody liked him."

Dennis Monday's son, Andy Monday, is a super late model driver on Thursday nights. He was fifteen years old when Pagel's fatal crash occurred.

"I wasn't on Jim's pit crew, per se, but I would accompany Dad to the shop and I really idolized Jim growing up," said Andy Monday. "He was a great sportsman for racing. Looking back, Jim was one of those guys that no matter what happened on the track, a good or a bad night, he was always in the same mood.

"I'd equate him with guys like Mike Gardner or John Meidam. They were one in the same; just very polite, professional-acting people. Sometimes when I want to get angry about something that happened on the track or I feel the urge to want to post something potentially negative on social media, I feel like I have Jim on my shoulder for guidance."

Accidents Mar Abbreviated Opening Night at WIR

May 3, 1997
(Reprinted from the Appleton Post-Crescent *with permission)*

By Tom Goff

A crowd of 3,750 was on hand Thursday looking forward with great anticipation to the first Fox River Racing Club late model feature race of the season at Wisconsin International Raceway in Kaukauna.

What they got instead was a horrific pre-race crash that took the life of veteran late model driver Jim Pagel early today.

They also witnessed a demolition derby of sorts in the feature race that mercifully ended on lap 18 when track officials threw the checkered flag after the sixth caution period.

At the end of it all the winner was Jim Weber, who is going through his own personal tragedy, facing second-degree reckless homicide charges in the shooting death of his hunting partner and friend Reno Spiegel.

"Any wins feel great, but if I ever needed a win to boost my morale this was it," said Weber, who passed Gordie Sannes Jr. on lap 12 and was still in front when the race was declared over.

"I just thank God that my crew, sponsors and everyone else is standing behind me through this tragedy and that includes the fans," added Weber.

A greasy track caused by fluids dropped by damaged cars as well as overanxious drivers contributed to a multitude of spins, off-track excursions and wrecks. The last such incident occurred when Sannes apparently blew an engine and collected several other cars, almost completely blocking turn three.

"Opening night doldrums," Weber said of the incidents. "Everyone was trying to get their cars working and they weren't sure out there."

Weber had his own problems in the Alan Kulwicki Memorial dash when his car slid going through a turn and spun, nearly taking Lowell Bennett with him.

"In the dash I bent a shock and it caused the wheel to hop. I thought I broke the brake rotor but we found it before the feature, and after that the car was awesome," he said of his red Chevrolet Monte Carlo.

Only half of the 20-car field was running at the end of the race.

Terry Baldry finished second in a Monte Carlo followed by Tom Spierowski in another Chevy and defending track champion Mark Schroeder in a Ford Thunderbird.

"A fiasco," was Schroeder's analysis of the evening. "You'd think after what happened (with Pagel) the guys would be more careful. There's more to life than these goofy cars."

Pagel's crash cast a pall on the night's events and it made it hard for the drivers to compete, according to Bennett. "It's hard. There's not much you can do except just keep saying prayers for him," he said. "This could happen to anyone of us at any time."

With all the spins and accidents and clean-up time, it took nearly an hour to complete the 18 laps. Under ordinary circumstances, with no yellow flags and cars turning around 20-second laps, that number of laps could conceivably be run in just over six minutes.

Chad Roffers won the 15-lap semi-feature. He and Dan Nettekoven, who finished second, transferred to the feature under a new policy adopted this year.

Earl Clement held off fast qualifier and 1989 champ Steve Smits by inches to win the 20-lap limited late model feature. Rookie Greg Wichman placed third.

Terry Van Roy was a double winner, taking the first 15-lap street stock feature and the 15-lap figure-8 race. Mike Rahn won the other street stock race.

Hank Calmes was the winner in the 18-lap Wisconsin Sport Truck feature, barely holding off defending track champion Andy Geiger.

Only Tough Questions Remain

May 4, 1997
(Reprinted from the Appleton Post-Crescent *with permission)*

By Tom Goff

Was Jim Pagel's death due to a freak racing accident, or did track negligence come into play?

Considering that there was water on the track, should the cars have been allowed to race at all, especially after the crash?

Was the Fox River Racing Club at fault? Or track owner Roger Van Daalwyk?

Those were some of the questions on everyone's mind following Thursday night's tragic crash that took the life of one of the club's most talented and well-liked drivers.

Pagel died as the result of massive head and chest injuries he sustained during a crash following his second qualifying lap when he lost control of his car at the end of the main straightaway and it hit the first-turn wall driver's side first at over 80 mph.

What caused the crash is a matter of conjecture, and nobody will ever know for sure.

Was it the water? Mechanical failure? Did a brush with the pit wall cause the spin? Did Pagel just lose control of his car? Or was it a combination of several factors?

Driver Jeff Frederickson, the next car in line to qualify after Pagel, says he believes water definitely was a factor in the crash.

"I saw the water spray up and so did everyone in my crew," he said. "We looked over the wall and you could see where his tire tracks went through the water. When he hit that water, his car turned around. There was nothing he could do."

Frederickson said he couldn't believe that some people were making light of the situation and was appalled that the race wasn't called off after what happened to Pagel. "Some of the guys were saying we should put up a sign saying 'no wake zone,'" he said. "This is not a joking matter. These cars are not designed to race on water."

Water seepage has been a problem at the track for the past four or five years, Van Daalwyk admits. And there was water on the track Thursday night along the white stripe marking the left edge of the track and also in the backstretch coming off turn two.

But because the water was not considered in the racing groove that is the two lanes where the cars normally race, track officials didn't think it would be a problem and allowed the event to continue.

"We had a guy taking measurements there today. He measured the skid marks past the start-finish line and from that, he determined (Pagel) wasn't even close to it (the water), or he couldn't have made the turn," Van Daalwyk said.

Van Daalwyk added that water in that location is not unusual because it runs into a drain located near the flagstand of the inner quarter-mile track.

Veteran drivers such as Lowell Bennett, Rod Wheeler and J.J. Smith frequently take a line on their last qualifying lap to get the maximum speed possible that puts them very close to the wall. But normally, they don't get that close to the white line when they qualify.

"There's usually a good half car length between the wall and you and normally you're not down there where the standing water is," said Wheeler.

Added Bennett, "You can't get that low or you won't make the corner if you pinch it that tight."

But Smith, who has been racing late models for 34 years at WIR, said that while drivers don't usually get that close to the white line, he has done so on several occasions.

"On the last lap sometimes you do get that close. The other thing is when you do the car will bobble down there because there's sand and debris laying down there too, so it's hard to say what happened," he said.

Van Daalwyk said he was also aware of the water on the backstretch.

"The water table is so high, it was coming through the asphalt, but it's not in the racing groove," he said. ""There's two and a half lanes above where the water was. If we had to race through it there's no way we would have raced."

But Chad Roffers, the driver of one of the cars waiting in line to qualify prior to the crash, said he did have to drive through the water on the backstretch. "We went out there for the semi-feature and heat race and there was a puddle coming out of turn two. If you were on the inside you really had to be careful. You had to hope the guy (on the outside) would give you enough room and not run your tires through the puddle. But I drove through it a couple of times and I got off the throttle. It was pretty scary," he said.

Despite the accident and the water, FRRC officials and Van Daalwyk didn't feel that calling off the program was warranted.

"We asked the drivers. A couple of them were concerned, but ever since I've been there there's always been water. It seeps up and you put oil dry on it. The thing was it got so cold, the whole thing was getting pretty damp and there was oil all over the track. That's why we ended the feature when we did," FRRC president Mike Clancy said. "Everybody can find fault after the fact, but we'd never intentionally send a car out if the conditions were unsafe," he added.

Ultimately, the final decision to call off a race is made by the club officials and Van Daalwyk. That happened during the first race of the Red, White and Blue series three years ago, when the race had to be postponed due to water on the track. "I remember we got five inches of rain the day before and it (the water) was coming out of the middle of turns one and two. It was a beautiful day, but the cars were spinning in qualifying and we had to stop it and call it off."

Some drivers speculated that a part on the car may have broken and caused the accident.

But Ken Des Jardin, who co-owned the car with Pagel, said that it didn't appear that mechanical failure had anything to do with the accident. "We looked at the car this morning and the suspension and everything seemed to be operating. We looked at the brake lines and the throttle linkage. Nothing failed," he said.

Pagel, who won rookie-of-the-year honors on both the quarter and half-mile tracks, and Des Jardin had been together racing for eight years. "I started with him on the quarter-mile. He was just like a brother to me. I'm just heartbroken," he said.

Another theory was that Pagel may have hit the end of the pit wall causing his car to spin. But Wheeler said he didn't think that happened. "I heard that, so I went over and looked at the wall, and there were no fresh marks on it," he said. "There was no red paint on it that we could see."

Pagel is only the second driver to die in a crash on the oval portion of the raceway's complex which also includes a dragstrip, and the first fatality in the weekly Thursday night program.

The only other death was on Aug. 1, 1981, when Larry Detjens of Wausau was killed in an accident during an ARTGO race.

The track, first known as KK Sports Arena, opened in 1964 as a dirt track. It was paved in 1968 and hasn't been replaced since, although Van Daalwyk said that plans could include repaving it this fall.

Generally speaking, most drivers agree that despite the water problems and the older racing surface, WIR is a safe place to race.

"Personally I don't think WIR is a very dangerous place to race," said Bennett, defending champ at Slinger Speedway and the 1991 FRRC champ. "The safety crew is far superior to a lot of tracks I've raced at, and I've been to a lot of tracks. But I think they need to put the "soft walls" up in both corners like they have coming off of turn four."

Soft walls are Styrofoam blocks that absorb energy at impact. "The cracks in the track are getting further apart and moisture lays in those cracks and some of that gets in trouble. But I see no need to repave the track," said Smith, the 1990 champ. "It's not that rough. There's some dips here and there but I don't think repaving it will make it any safer."

Smith said he was involved in a similar crash to Pagel's at the speedway.

"It was 10 or 15 years ago. I had a very similar crash. I went into the wall driver's side first and the impact is unbelievable. You just can't realize what it's like. And it happened in about the same place that Jim Pagel's did," he said.

Jim Pagel after a 1996 victory. (www.danlewisphoto.net)

Randy Gintner after a victory in 1998. (www.danlewisphoto.net)

Detroit Iron
True Parity

The sportsman division at Wisconsin International Raceway in the 1970s and early 1980s just as well could have been dubbed "Detroit Iron."

For the most part, the cars were tough – made of real, original sheet metal from the manufacturing plants in Lower Michigan. The cars were real Chevrolet Camaros, real Pontiac Firebirds, real Ford Mustangs, real Dodge Darts. Unlike the cookie cutter-looking machines of the modern era, the sportsman class had true parity.

"It just seemed like everybody put all their own stuff together back then," said Appleton's Bill Fischer, who launched his racing career on the flat quarter-mile in 1983. "There was a lot of ingenuity back then and the cars were identifiable."

Fischer got a call one day from Dan Devine, a car owner in Mackville.

"His driver, Ross Goldbeck, was drilling wells in Minnesota so he couldn't make it," said Fischer. "Dan told me, 'We're bringing Ross's car to WIR and you're going to race it.' That's how I got started. I brought my motorcycle helmet and used that, and raced in a t-shirt and shorts. We didn't wear racing gloves or anything like that like they do now."

Because the cars were very affordable, the sportsman class was never lacking for car count.

"There were times we'd have more than fifty cars," recalled Fischer. "For a while, it seemed like we'd have two semi-features."

Fischer's last season as a driver was 1997. He continues to help out on Thursday nights working as a pit steward.

Dave Van Elzen in 1981. (Gary Vercauteren photo)

Dave Van Elzen's "Detroit Iron" was a blue 1972 Nova, built and driven for years by Kaukauna dirt late model legend Pete Parker. 1980 was Van Elzen's year to shine, as he shattered the track record qualifying laps at not only WIR, but also dirt tracks at Shawano and Luxemburg – all with that same old Nova.

"We did real well in points that year, too," said Van Elzen, a Kimberly native who now lives in Sherwood. "We won the championships at Shawano and Luxemburg, and got either second or third at Kaukauna. And we stayed busy going three nights a week, with two of those nights being with the same car switching over from asphalt to dirt."

Van Elzen got his start by pitting for Parker for a season and learning a lot.

"Pete (Parker's) pit crew that year was me, Ron Van Roy and Pete's dad, Mel," said Van Elzen. "Roger Van Roy had that Nova for a while, and then

Frank Van Oudenhoven drove it as a late model a couple of years later."

Van Elzen was able to squeeze enough speed out of that Nova, especially on Thursday nights.

"At Kaukauna, I had fast time six out of the thirteen nights we ran," said Van Elzen. "We were running so fast one time that summer that Mike Randerson came over and said, 'Bring that car over to my shop. I'd like to scale it sometime.'"

The work to convert the car from asphalt to dirt would start at the track on Thursday nights.

"As people would be drinking beer around our pit, we'd be pulling the windshield out and replacing it with a screen for Shawano," said Van Elzen. "We'd put the dirt tires on right at WIR that night, too. Then on Saturday nights at Shawano, we'd have to switch transmissions to race at Luxemburg the following night. It kept us busy."

Van Elzen tangled with Jim Duchow one night at WIR.

"I remember that crash because Chuck Grall drove underneath my car when I was flying through the air," said Van Elzen. "It was a bad wreck, and when I went to work on Friday, we were real busy and I didn't think we'd be able to make it to Shawano Saturday with all the repairs we had to make."

Van Elzen received a pleasant surprise when he returned home from work Friday.

"My pit crew had gone out to Clyde Schumacher's junkyard to get the parts we needed to get it fixed," said Van Elzen. "We made it out to Shawano just as time trials were getting wrapped up. We rolled through the gates and their race director, Corny (Schmidt), told me, 'You've got five minutes to get this thing unloaded and get a qualifying lap in.' I see Mike Panure (one of Van Elzen's top competitors at Shawano) leaning against the inner guardrail. I asked Mike, 'How's it going?' He replied, 'I just set the track record with a 26 seconds flat lap.' We unloaded our beat-up Nova from Thursday night, took a lap and broke his track record with a 25.9. Then I saw Panure climb back into his car and try to get his track record back, but it didn't happen."

1980 turned out to be profitable for Van Elzen, as he actually made a little bit of money racing when all of the bills were paid at year's end.

"That was a fun year, and at Kaukauna it seemed like I was starting in the back row every week," said Van Elzen. "Guys like Chuck Grall always seemed to start in the front row week after week."

It was in 1980 when the club began implementing a rule that the previous week's feature winner needed to start in the back of feature starting lineup. That rule was put in, in part, to help eliminate drivers from "sandbagging" or purposely qualifying at a slower speed to get a better starting spot for the features.

Van Elzen raced two more seasons after his big year and stepped away from racing in 1983 to build his home in Sherwood. His racing career on the quarter-mile resumed in 1989. He retired again in 2000 when the sportsman class moved to the half-mile.

"I was against those cars moving to the half-mile because it just cost too much money," said Van Elzen. He's continued to coach middle school football for the Sherwood Lions football club for nearly a quarter of a century. "I love working with kids."

***

Darboy's Dennis Dietzen was a champion on the quarter-mile in 1976 and 1986 at WIR. Dietzen got his start racing in the Figure 8 class with Dave Valentyne.

"I bought a Plymouth Coupe from Jerry Meyer in '66," said Dietzen. "Everything came out of the junkyard, so racing was affordable then."

The flat quarter-mile made it very tough for drivers to pass.

"Sometimes in a feature, we'd have fourteen cars and nobody moved," said Dietzen. "Wherever you started, that's where you ended up. It was so close."

Championship points were tough to get because of the limited passing. After a time, points were awarded for top qualifiers in time trials.

"That was also done to help prevent sandbagging," said Dietzen, who was Fox River Racing Club vice president four years and treasurer for six years.

"I got involved with helping run the club just to help chip in. It seemed like we had a real good spirit of cooperation back then. It's a little bit different now."

Dietzen hung up his helmet after the 1987 season. "It was still somewhat affordable even when we got out of racing," said Dietzen. "I remember we ran an entire season and only bought eight tires."

Kurt Johnson, another sportsman competitor, got thrown into the fire as FRCC club president in just his second year of racing in 1980.

"I got it handed off to me because nobody seemed to want to deal with the headaches at the time," said Johnson, from Oshkosh. "But truthfully, it did sort of run itself. They had guys lined up to work with (WIR owner) Joe (Van Daalwyk), so it wasn't really that bad. We basically dealt with and maintained the growth the club was experiencing."

As for his own racing career, Johnson got involved in racing through two other racers – Pete Weyenberg and John Geske.

"Geske worked for my dad and I bugged those guys in the shop, hanging around and being on their pit crews," said Johnson.

Johnson's first time behind the wheel was 1979 driving a Ford.

"The first year I was in everybody's way," joked Johnson, who's racing career ended in 1984 when he won the track title. "The tough guys were Pete Berken, Dennis Dietzen, Jim Duchow, and Jeff Herrmann."

Johnson was heading the FRRC ship when the 9:1 compression rule for late model motors was implemented across Wisconsin, including WIR.

"Bob Abitz was the vice president then, and he sort of went and ran with it as he was our tech inspector," said Johnson. "He had all the tools and that. He had gotten out of racing himself."

Johnson did his two-year term, with Al Golueke, Ray Dietzen and Donny Hauser the other board members.

Johnson's last year racing was 1984, when he won the track championship. His biggest on-track rivalry was with Berken.

"We traded paint more than once," quipped Johnson, who sported car number 74 because 1974 was the year he graduated from high school.

***

Neenah's Rick Spoo got his racing start in the sportsman class as a crew member for Kurt Johnson.

"I went to the races when I was younger and I really enjoyed it," said Spoo. "I helped build cars with Kurt and eventually I started my own racing career."

Rick Spoo (left) and Kurt Johnson at an FRRC awards banquet. (Rick Spoo collection)

Spoo chose number 24 because that was his age when he started racing in the mid-1980s. He quickly found success, winning the track titles in 1987, 1990 and 1991.

"I remember Steve Smits being a real tough competitor to run with," recalled Spoo.

Spoo was voted Sportsman Racer of the Year after the 1990 season by the group Wisconsin Fans for Auto Racing.

"That was a real big deal back then," explained Spoo. "They'd have a real nice banquet they'd invite you to down in Milwaukee. It was real classy."

After winning his 1991 quarter-mile crown, Spoo made the bold move up to the half-mile and the late model class.

"It was a whole new creature," explained Spoo. "I didn't have the success that I had on the quarter-mile. The biggest expense moving up is motor and tires. The tire rule just got out of hand. When I started out, it was unlimited tires. There were guys running six tires a night. Guys would start up front and they'd put on brand new right sides for the tires. It was crazy."

When drivers race late models on the half-mile, most have a "keeping up with the Joneses" mentality and feel the need to buy big, fancy enclosed trailers – even if they only live minutes from the track. Not Spoo.

"I was one of the few half-mile guys toward the end who still towed my car there with an open trailer," said Spoo. "The trailer doesn't make you go any faster. I still have it to this day."

Spoo packed away his driver's suit and retired after 2003.

"They were switching the concept to an ACE motor. I did not see things going that way. I was short on sponsors and it was just time to get out," he said.

***

Kurt Johnson wasn't the only sportsman driver loyal to Ford's "Blue Oval."

When the Gintner brothers – Tom, Randy and Larry – grew up in Neenah, their dad, Robert, would prefer that any visitors driving a Chevrolet or any other non-Ford vehicle park in the road and not his driveway.

"Dad wasn't a racer himself, but was always a diehard Ford guy," said Tom Gintner. "So us three brothers always ran nothing but Ford stuff our entire racing careers. Running Fords was engrained in us. There was not another option, it seemed."

"If it wasn't for Dad, none of us would ever have taken up racing," said Randy Gintner. "While he never raced, he was always helping us on the pit crews and stuff."

Tom and Randy started out racing on the dirt at Leo's Speedway in Oshkosh – Tom in 1973 and Randy in 1977.

"I remember they called a meeting for the rookies underneath the grandstand before the '77 season, and I'm sitting next to Alan Kulwicki of all people," recalled Randy. "I had a '64 Ford Galaxy and rolled it over that year. I ran it on the asphalt at WIR and I also ran it on the dirt half-mile at

Seymour. That was my one and only year on the dirt."

Tom and Larry wheeled Ford Mustangs and Torinos throughout the years. The brothers always kept detailed records and receipts of what they were spending on their fast-paced hobby.

"One year, when I ran after all the bills were paid, I wound up making a $25 profit," said Larry Gintner. "I kept real close records of what I spent and what I made."

Randy Gintner actually turned a profit racing the Ford Mustang.

"I paid $1,000 for it, and that season I ran it I took in $1,800 in prize money," boasted Gintner. "I got my money's worth out of it. Every year I'd do stuff to update it. I'd take a car that ran 18-second laps and I got it down to a 15.5 lap time. My theory always was you should be building the car from scratch to save money. That's what I did. I had a family to raise and house payments and stuff. I wasn't going to go broke racing, that's for sure. My philosophy was you should build it from a boneyard versus a speed shop."

The sportsman class was moved up to the half-mile in 2001. Randy's tired old piece of iron just couldn't compete on the bigger track with the newer, tricked-out chassis.

"It would have cost between 10 to 18 thousand dollars for us, on average, to move up (to the half-mile), so we decided against it," said Randy Gintner. "The last year, 2001, I ran at Columbus 151 Speedway."

WIR Sportsman Drivers List - 1985

0	Jim Belling	Larsen	'84 Firebird
03	Wally Blank	Menasha	'83 Fairmont
04	Pete Berken	Appleton	'85 Camaro
05	Dick Willing	Appleton	'85 Thunderbird
07	Robin Boegh	Menasha	'83 Mirada
1	Randy Boegh	Appleton	'84 Firebird
2	Jim Duchow	Kaukauna	'84 Camaro
3	Don Hauser	Little Chute	'84 Thunderbird
4	Dan Meisenhelder	Kaukauna	'81 Camaro
5	Rod Wheeler	Appleton	'85 Firebird
6	Gary Stankevitz	Green Bay	'78 Firebird
7	Ran Schmoeker	Kaukauna	'82 Camaro
8	Mike Kasparek	Tigerton	'70 Chevelle
V8	G.M. Cobb	Menasha	'68 Camaro
9	Todd Herrmann	Kaukauna	'81 Camaro
10	Mark Anthony	Appleton	'81 Camaro
12	Russell Keberlein	Kaukauna	'81 Camaro
14	Gene Steinfeldt	Appleton	'72 Nova
15	Jerry Smits	Appleton	'73 Mustang
16	Steve Henry	Appleton	'82 AMC Spirit
17	Mick Hopensberger	Menasha	'65 Chevelle
18	Jack Hardy	Appleton	'81 Camaro
20	Gary Sieg	Appleton	'85 Camaro
22	Mark Vandenboogard	Little Chute	'83 Firebird
24	Rick Spoo	Neenah	'85 Buick Regal
25	Krisanne Haufschildt	Wrightstown	'79 Cutlass
26	Horse Haufschildt	Wrightstown	'81 Grand Prix
27	Dwayne Maroszek	Hortonville	'81 Camaro
30	Tommy Raatz	Appleton	'81 Camaro
31	Russ Wagner	Little Suamico	'84 Firebird

Cont.

32	Gil Wagner	Green Bay	'84 Camaro
33	Randy Rasmussen	Little Chute	'84 Monte Carlo
34	Jerry Wenzel	Two Rivers	'81 Camaro
40	Ross Goldbeck	Appleton	'83 Cordoba
44	Bill Fischer	Appleton	'85 Camaro
45	Dennis Utke	Kimberly	'81 Camaro
47	Don Allard	Appleton	'81 Camaro
50	Jim Anthony	Kaukauna	'85 Firebird
52	Ron Bomber	Green Bay	'81 Camaro
54	Jim King	Appleton	'70 Mustang
57	Gary Beattie	Menasha	'68 Camaro
59	Kevin Danley	Black Creek	'72 Monte Carlo
62	Dan Petermann	Brillion	'71 Camaro
66	Mark Vandenberg	Menasha	'78 Cutlass
67	Dennis Dietzen	Appleton	'83 Thunderbird
69	David Vandenheuvel	Appleton	'80 Camaro
73	Kurt Schweitzer	Appleton	'84 Firebird
76	Tony Pues	Neenah	'83 Camaro
77	Dave Sanders	Kaukauna	'83 Camaro
78	Bryce Spoehr	Black Creek	'76 Ventura
79	Jeff Herrmann	Branch	'85 Firebird
83	Daniel Dekleyn	Appleton	'78 Nova
85	Steve Mueller	Manitowoc	'85 Firebird
87	Ken Waszisczko	Hilbert	'85 Thunderbird
88	Doug Carpenter	Appleton	'77 Chevelle
90	Larry Gintner	Neenah	'66 Mustang
95	Brent Ward	Little Chute	'69 Chevelle
96	Steve Smits	De Pere	'81 Camaro
97	Dave Wypiszynski	De Pere	'85 Monte Carlo
98	Jeff Belongea	Kaukauna	'81 Camaro
99	Randy Gintner	Menasha	'73 Mustang

JJ Smith with his dedicated pavement car. (Bob Bergeron photo)

Nuts and Bolts
WIR's Bits and Pieces

In the course of researching a book as wide-ranging as this, inevitably there will be stories and individual interviews that might not fit in existing chapters or merit one of their own. That's what we have here. The following segments feature some of the best-known personalities in Wisconsin International Raceway history, and the story of the facility would not be complete without their contributions.

Dave Marcis – Wausau, Wisconsin
Veteran Winston Cup driver. Won the USAC stock car race at WIR in 1972.

"I remember how cool it was that at the time we finally had a half-mile paved track in Wisconsin. I had been running tracks at the Dells, Tomah-Sparta, Stratford and Tomahawk, so I really thought KK was big then. When I ran NASCAR at Talladega and Daytona, it really put things into perspective. I moved down south in 1969. Back then if you wanted to race full time, it was either USAC or NASCAR. I had no real family that was into racing back then.

"When we won that USAC race, Dave Deppe owned the car. I recall the USAC officials really giving us a hard time that day, because we were fast. Bill Bembinster from BEMCO built that car. It was a Chevy Nova with a 350 in it. We took advantage of the weight break they gave us."

Dave Deppe – Baraboo, Wisconsin
Car owner for several drivers, including Dave Marcis

"The day of that USAC race we were fast, real fast. The USAC boys didn't like that. Bill (Bembinster) at BEMCO had a habit of making stuff just about as close as you could make it or stretch it. He built that car with a chassis that went below the rear axle. USAC officials didn't like that. They gave us a real hard time in tech before the race. Then when Dave won, he lapped the field all the way up to fifth. The USAC hot dogs at the time, Butch Hartman and Don White, they were pretty upset that a Wisconsin local beat up on them.

"We had a NASCAR driver with a ragtag pit crew thrown together, and we flat out dusted them. They had us in the parking lot for two hours teching afterwards. I still ran a couple of USAC shows after that, but they were always trying to find something wrong with it. I was so pissed at USAC because they were always sweating us that I finally sold the car. But she was fast."

Greg "Doogie" Hauser – Little Chute, Wisconsin
Second-generation driver. Super stock track champion in 2007 and 2014

"Roger Regeth was actually a big help in getting me started with my first race car in 1997. Mainly shocks and springs and stuff. My first car was a 1971 Buick Skylark. I've always tried to take pride in my race cars and how they look. (Hauser is a body man by trade with Hauser's Auto Frame and Body). Dad always told me, 'There are enough people that bring junk to the race track, so there's no need to bring any more.' I try to live up to that. They get a little beat up toward the end of the year.

"The key to staying competitive on the quarter-mile is being comfortable in your equipment. I built the car new in 2007 and just keep updating it as time goes on. You'd think you'd have to run the outside to get to the front, but we won the title by passing 90 percent of the cars on the bottom. It changes.

"I like this class. You don't have to take it quite as seriously. I ran the half-mile in a limited late model for a couple of years. I put too much pressure on myself. So this is a better fit for me."

Mike Clancy – Kaukauna, Wisconsin
FRRC president 1996 and 1997 and sponsor of several racers

"I used to help Roger Regeth, JJ Smith, Jerry Smith and LeeRoy Meverden. LeeRoy drove the 53 car. He wrecked at De Pere and brought the car to my shop in Wrightstown. We started early in the morning and finished the car later that day. I've sponsored Jeff (Van Oudenhoven) for many years, too.

"Dave Valentyne talked me into running for club president. I really liked it. We tried to treat everybody right down the way. When I was president, we'd have close to forty late models some nights. We took over $500,000 in revenue those years. We paid out a sizeable point fund, insurance for half a year, and were always in real good shape financially.

"We had a good crew with Fred Pagel, Mitch Heimlich and Jerry Quella. They all had a job. We really didn't have any glitches. I enjoyed everything about it. I loved getting involved and I was always trying to get racers more money. I'd go up to Norway (Michigan) and give some of them free pit passes to come, because I knew they had a long ways to drive. And they'd come back the next week then, so that worked. We'd get some Slinger guys that came, too."

Ron Van Roy – Darboy, Wisconsin
1972 President of the Fox Valley Stock Car Club. Former Fox River Racing Club board member. Father of Figure 8 and super stock champion Terry Van Roy.

"It really was tough sledding for the (FRRC) club in the early days. When we got to be officers, there were only ten or so guys who came to the meetings. We talked to Joe (Van Daalwyk) about coming back to the track. We ran for 50 percent of the gate. We had to cut the half-mile cars at

28 seconds. There were not a lot of cars and not a lot of good payout. Joe agreed to back our guaranteed payout. At the end of the year, Joe would get 25 percent of the profit. There was no profit. After some time, that guaranteed payout slowly built the car count up. It drew better cars. That drew (Larry) Schuler and those guys.

"We pretty much donated our services. Some of us maybe got paid $25 a night for multiple nights. I thought if you didn't have a race car, you should donate your time. I got out of being a vice president. I want to say I got out of in after 1978 or so. We were able to build it up. The guaranteed payoff made it successful. The club was down to nobody. Eventually it made it to a lot of cars. When I quit in '78, there was a strong number of cars. Richie Somers and "Reegie" (Roger Regeth) and Schuler and those guys came every week. That's what made it successful."

On the Van Roy and Gracyalny rivalry: "It wasn't a real good relationship years ago. It was about Dan (Gracyalny) and Terry (Van Roy) in the Figure 8s initially. But Terry got along with Dave (Gracyalny). We always had differences of opinions on how rules were enforced. It got a little testy once in a while. When Randy (Van Roy) married Jessie (Gracyalny), it sort of smoothed things over."

Jeff Van Oudenhoven – Appleton, Wisconsin

Five-time super late model track champion. Came back from a horrific wreck in 2015 where he broke his ankle and won the 2016 track title and three Red, White and Blue titles. Van Oudenhoven and Rod Wheeler are the only drivers to have won track titles on both the quarter-mile and the half-mile. His current car owners are Scott Vandenheuvel and former sportsman driver Terry Korth.

"My first year racing was 1991 on the quarter-mile. My car owner was Rick Marx. My mom and dad (Milo Van Oudenhoven, former racer and WIR track official) never even knew Rick bought me this car. Rick had a shop and we had to put some lights in there. Rick and my parents' neighbor, who was a millwright, wired up some fluorescent lighting for the shop. He brought my dad down and there he was. Dad thought it would cost a lot of money and take a lot of time. My mom was 100 percent behind it.

"I wasn't even born when Dad raced. Dad was the pit steward there when the track started. He was in there before that with my grandpa. They were related to Roger Ward, who ran Indy Car. Dad ran the IMCA circuit years and years ago, and he really enjoyed it.

"As far as the crash went, it happens. You maybe get a bad wreck like that every ten years. These cars are way safer than street cars."

Bryce Spoehr – Black Creek, Wisconsin
Raced sportsman up until his age matched his car number 78. The last year he raced was 1999. His son, Gary Spoehr, was a longtime crew member.

"Dad took second in the points on two different occasions to Pete Berken on the final night of the season, and the other year they still ran coupes he took second to Ron Van Roy. That was in 1974. My dad and his longtime crew chief, Cal Breitrick, bought an old Terry Baldry car from Ron and Wally Blank. That was the first car they didn't build themselves. Same thing went for the motors. They always built everything on their own. I mean everything.

"Dad was proudest of not taking any money from the family budget. It was money that he earned doing odd jobs or other things, even money he made through racing. When Dad stopped driving truck in the mid '80s, I started to help him out and we'd begin getting some sponsor money. Before they'd let us buy a tire, even a nut and bolt, I had to promise them that I wasn't taking any money out of my pocket to buy it. I think the most money we ever had in a year was $1,700. That included Tim's Auto Body who painted the car and bought us four tires for the car. Tim was our biggest sponsor.

"The most cash we ever got from one sponsor was $500. Bryce and Cal scrimped and saved. The best engine they ever had took Cal over a year to assemble all the parts. Cal ran a gas station in Hortonville. Every car that needed engine work, he'd take the pistons out. He'd weigh them and measure them. He found one set from different pistons from different engines. He built an engine out of that. Basically everybody's cast-off stuff. They even built their own brakes one year – even the drums. They were very resourceful.

"When I was growing up, my brother and I would sell the *Midwest Racing News* and *Checkered Flag Racing News* at Leo's Speedway (in Oshkosh) and Kaukauna. The Vercauterens came in and then I'd sell papers for them. They gave me a jacket and everything, and took me to some tracks I'd never been to before. It was a really neat time back then."

JJ Smith – Appleton, Wisconsin
After many feature wins and championships on the local dirt tracks, Smith committed to running the pavement at WIR full time in the 1982 season. He won his only late model track title driving for the Anthony Brothers of Appleton in 1990.

"I really enjoyed racing the dirt, but the cars had really become two different animals in the early '80s. You couldn't do it anymore with the same car. The technology just sort of took over. Nowadays, you really have to have a pit crew that is on top of things and stays ahead of the game on the pavement. And the sponsors – they are a lot tougher to get now than they were back then. I was fortunate to drive for some really good car owners over the years."

Brett Van Horn – De Pere, Wisconsin
Won the Sport Truck titles from 2013 to 2016. Won a division-record 12 features in a row.

"When it comes to our success, it's really a combination of things. We've got a really good truck design from John Roeser and Dean Daul. They pretty much designed the whole chassis. We've had only three DNFs (did not finish) in six years of racing. We're pretty proud of that accomplishment, and frankly it's one of the reasons for our title run.

"Racing on that quarter-mile at WIR can be a rough ride. If you can run at WIR, you can be fast pretty much anywhere. Gordie Sannes is my uncle and godfather. I run number 36. Gordie was number 37. His son, Neal, was number 38, so I decided to go the other way when it came to picking a number for my truck."

Jim and John Anthony – Appleton, Wisconsin
The brothers have owned race teams at WIR for more than forty years. Their first year fielding a late model team on the half-mile produced their only track championship with JJ Smith in 1990.

"I actually started out pitting for Dewey Forbeck and then later Cliff Ebben," said John Anthony. "I was sixteen back then. My brother, Jim, owned cars with me and then my brother-in-law, Dick Willing, got involved. We had Dave Watson drive our car, along with Ebben, JJ (Smith) and Rod Wheeler. My nephew, Travis Willing, raced a little bit on the quarter-mile. In fact, we still hold the track record on the quarter-mile for the sportsman class with Rod.

"I've had RanderCar chassis the whole time over the years. I worked for a while for (Ebben). I even went to Speedweeks with him down in Florida one time when he was running the dirt late model. I was on his pit crew. That was one of the coolest things I did. When JJ retired, my son, Michael, sort of took over running our car. We've had a lot of wrecks over the years. Racing is in our blood."

Marty Nussbaum – Kaukauna, Wisconsin
Superfan and unofficial track historian. Has perfect attendance for every single Fox River Racing Club event since the first event held on June 12, 1975.

"My uncle is Rene Grode and my dad, Ray Nussbaum, served as an assistant flagman and then flagman for a while. I was hooked after my first time at WIR. As the years went on, I would serve on the FRRC board, assist the tech officials, became an assistant flagman and a race car owner. Someday I wouldn't mind a crack at being flagman at the track. I can't think of any other place I'd rather be on a Thursday night than at WIR."

George Giesen – Menasha, Wisconsin
Giesen, now 84, won the first race run at WIR on the half-mile when it was a dirt track.

"It was quite a thrill because I had fast time that day, too, and that was a pretty big deal. I also ran the first race when they paved the track in 1968. In that first paved race, I had a '67 Plymouth with a 426 cubic inch wedge in it. Roger "The Bear" Regeth was running a car for Al Piette that day. We'd mix it up a lot together. We traded a lot of paint. We're friends today. I beat Dick Trickle out here one year with that Plymouth. I got a taste of going a little faster, so I started running the USAC stock car shows across the Midwest."

Joe Shear – Clinton, Wisconsin
Four-time Red White and Blue state champion. Died of cancer March 6, 1998, at age 54.

Shear won an estimated 350 short track events in his career, including four of his last five races. However, his long time car owner, Fred Neilsen, estimated Shear won closer to 600 events in his career. He was a driver who also had a reputation for nailing down fast time on many occasions. Shear was an ARTGO champion in 1986 and 1989. His son, Joe Shear Jr., has worked down south for a number of NASCAR teams as a crew chief, most recently for Johnny Sauter.

Joe Shear in 1980
(Gary Vercauteren photo)

Car owners Jerry and Jeff Korinek (left) pose with crew member Mark Sawyer next to their mini champ racer at a 2016 vintage car show in Freedom, Wis. (Joe Verdegan photo)

Mini Champs and Trucks
Gentlemen, Pull Your Recoils

When 141 Speedway in Francis Creek closed after the 1987 season, the JKJ mini champs were a class of race cars without a home track to race on. The open-wheel machines, powered by snowmobile engines, had been running weekly at the Francis Creek oval for several seasons. The group had run special events at Wisconsin International Raceway over the years, in particular the Budweiser 500 in September.

The mini champs never needed a huge payout, making them a popular draw for race promoters since they didn't break the bank. In 1975, Jerry and Jeff Korinek of Manitowoc, along with Ken Konop, a teacher from Brillion, formed a corporation called JKJ Inc. to manage the group. The group ran at 141 Speedway beginning in 1975. The early mini champs ran DOT-legal tires you could buy at Fleet Farm, for example – no racing tires.

"The key with this was to make it reasonable and competitive in nature," said Jerry Korinek.

At its peak, the group had more than forty drivers registered hailing from communities such as Manitowoc (Greg Martell, Jimbo Schleis, Paul Baroun and the Korineks), Two Rivers (Pete Shambeau and Jerry Brickner), Brillion (Pete Zarnoth and Konop), New Franken (Kevin Servais), De Pere (Bob Smits), Green Bay (Ron Bomber), and Freedom (Hank Calmes, Bill and Dean Daul).

JKJ worked out the first arrangement with the Fox River Racing Club to race at WIR under the guidance of Dave Valentyne, a former club president.

"Dave is genuine, honest, and just plain loves racing, and a true gentleman," said Jerry Korinek. "The first year in 1987, Dave requested we only appear every other week as he had another specialty show that he also featured bi-weekly. After that year, we were contracted to appear weekly on Thursday nights at WIR."

Racing at WIR continued as mini champs for several years. FRRC later ran into some opposition from the insurance carrier about the mini champs actually being an open-wheel style of vehicle verses everything else at the track was full-bodied. FRRC management also wanted to promote a small truck series, and it organized a core group of folks from the Valley who wished to go in this direction.

Enter Appleton's Jerry Quella . The year was 1995.

"Back then, the mini champs were causing quite a few cautions and one of the big reasons was the open wheels," said Quella, who then was vice president of the FRRC. "Steve Giese was one who got the ball rolling about putting bodies on the trucks."

Quella wound up making a front end out of wood and cut some cardboard out to design a prototype body.

"Mike Schneider (eventual truck champion) took that to one of the club meetings," said Quella. "I remember we didn't give them a whole lot of time. This was right after the '95 season ended and we pretty much told them they had to put bodies on them. This was right up until after Christmas time. Some guys bought go kart bodies. They couldn't get anything to work initially. The biggest thing was we didn't want anything with the roll cages sticking out of the car."

Eventually, a truck body was developed that was scaled down from a commercially available body. The concept piggybacked off of NASCAR's newly formed Craftsman truck series.

With the conversion of the mini champs to the truck bodies, Korinek and his brother, Jeff, decided to retire from the circuit. Korinek won a season title once without ever winning a feature.

"Our belief then was that with the open wheels, it forced the drivers to have more respect for one another and be better drivers because of it," Jerry Korinek said. "We still believed in the overall concept of affordable racing and wanted to see it continue. So with that as a guide, we picked who we felt was the most qualified person to continue the process and turned the operation over to Hank Calmes, who like Dave Valentyne is a fine gentleman and extremely honest and fair."

Once Korinek stepped away, Calmes ran the association as a club, and according to Korinek "did very well" in taking care of it during his time. After Calmes' tenure was done, the club developed into the Wisconsin Sport Trucks as it is known today.

***

Initially, not everyone was in total agreement to go the route of the truck bodies. One of them was Calmes.

"The old mini champs were a lot of fun," said Calmes. "We could design them with wings and any downforce we could make. They wanted to go as fast as possible. And we could get real creative with the bodies. The rules allowed you basically to do whatever you had to do to get more downforce."

What's more, Calmes enjoyed traveling and racing against a group of mini champ drivers out of the Chicago area.

"They had more of an open rules deal where they could run three carbs, three pipes and they weighed a little more," said Calmes. "They came to Kaukauna and thought they were gonna really whoop up on us, but we stomped them. Their home track was La Crosse and we whooped up on them there, too. After the races they were commenting, 'Who invited these guys anyways?' "

Calmes remembers racing indoors at the MECCA in Milwaukee when the promoters put Coke syrup on the track as an adhesive.

The truck bodies were slower – a full second slower on WIR's quarter-mile.

"They were pushing a lot of wind with those bodies," recalled Calmes, who won a pair of track championships at WIR, including his last season in 2002. "I was going to hang it up after 2001 because I wound up seventh in points. Guys were saying I was old and fat and couldn't do the job anymore. So I had to prove them wrong."

Those comments, combined with the opportunity to race the trucks against his son, Kyle Calmes, for one season in 2002 motivated Calmes to race one more year and win the championship.

"That year I won the WIR title, the 141 traveling championship, and the King of Kings race, too," he said. "It was a good way to go out."

More Fox Valley drivers got involved with the division into the late 1990s as the trucks evolved and grew. In addition to Kyle Calmes from Freedom, Fox Valley drivers Andy and Bryan Monday, John Meidam, Todd Verhagen and Scott Baker all ran the trucks. Those drivers eventually would move up to race either late models or super late models on the track's half-mile.

***

When the trucks came on the scene, two drivers – Appleton's Mike Schneider and Brillion's Andy Geiger – dominated the truck championships from 1996 through 1999. Geiger won the crown in '96, with Schneider winning the next two seasons and Geiger returning to the champion's podium in 1999.

"Andy (Geiger) was one of the first guys to really get the hang of flexing those chassis with the truck bodies and making them go," recalled Schneider, who started out running mini champs in 1990. "He was really able to loosen those trucks up."

Schneider began dominating the division after hooking up with local snowmobile enthusiast Jeff Ludwig of Freedom.

"My most productive years were in '97 and '98, when I hooked up with Jeff (Ludwig)," said Schneider. "I know I had sixty-three total wins with heats and features. I remember we were winning so much I started giving all the trophies away to the kids."

In the end, when it came to the mini champ versus truck debate, Schneider was one for the trucks.

"Trucks were more like a real race car, you might say," said Schneider. "The mini champs were okay, but you were limited as to what you could do with those things. Clutches and motors were what made those things go faster. Most of the framework and stuff on them – you could build them certain ways. If you didn't know that much about building stuff, it was really tough. With the trucks you could adjust things like technology into the wheels and stuff. Four-wheel brakes. We changed the tires. We put little racing tires on them and they could last pretty much the whole year."

***

Pete Zarnoth (Joe Verdegan photo)

Brillion's Pete Zarnoth was attending the races as a fan at 141 Speedway late in the 1980 season.

"I saw the mini champs buzzing around the track and I told the wife, 'I've got to get one of those,' " said Zarnoth, a barber in Brillion. "She said, 'You'd better get yourself a good one then.' "

"The Flyin' Barber," as he is affectionately known, bought a car from Jim Kocourek. At the age of forty-eight, Zarnoth became a rookie in the mini champs and has raced every year since. At the age of eighty-four, he's still going strong.

"I made all the races at WIR up until 2015," said Zarnoth, who still races on occasion at Norway (Michigan) Speedway. "The truck is the same type of car we ran as the mini champ. I like the trucks personally, and it feels more like you're in a car. They are safer this way in my opinion."

Zarnoth is one to skimp and save, cutting costs on his ride whenever possible.

"I've only run two different bodies the entire time I've run the trucks," said Zarnoth, who tows his racer with his Buick Park Avenue and a modest snowmobile trailer. "I still enjoy tinkering with them. I think doing that even surpasses the racing part of it."

Zarnoth is quick to give pointers and advice to newcomers in the sport.

"I always tell these kids that it's much better for you if you're closer to the guy next to you," explained Zarnoth. "But these trucks are safe. I've had guys run right up in the back of me and go right over the top."

Mini Champs champions
1988 – Jeff Korinek
1989 – Bill Daul
1990 – Bill Daul
1991 – Jeff Korinek
1992 – Mike Springstroh
1993 – Mike Springstroh
1994 – Hank Calmes
1995 – Andy Geiger

Trucks champions
1996 – Andy Geiger
1997 – Mike Schneider
1998 – Mike Schneider
1999 – Andy Geiger
2000 – Robyn Wussow
2001 – Robyn Wussow
2002 – Hank Calmes
2003 – Dan Hansen
2004 – Jason Van Handel
2005 – Todd Schuette
2006 – Dan Vixmer
2007 – Dan Vixmer
2008 – Ron Magdanz
2009 – Ron Magdanz
2010 – Jason Plutz
2011 – John Roeser
2012 – Bryan Monday
2013 – Brett Van Horn
2014 – Brett Van Horn
2015 – Brett Van Horn
2016 – Brett Van Horn
2017 – Kyle Quella
2018 – Jason Plutz
2019 – Kyle Quella
2020 – Cody Vanderloop

Crowds pack the WIR grandstands for an Eve of Destruction event. (Roger Van Daalwyk collection)

Eve of Destruction
Better Get an Early Seat

Mike Bunnell, a regular Figure 8 driver from Neenah, approached Roger Van Daalwyk in 1998 about running some sort of Figure 8 special event at Wisconsin International Raceway.

"My first thought was how on earth can we make a Figure 8 race stand on its own?" questioned Van Daalwyk. "We tried it, and that was the beginning of the Eve of Destruction."

"The Eve" is an event where cars get wrecked, burned and crushed. Novelty races such as chain races, Double 00 races and two-man cruiser events are the headliners.

"People like to see stuff get wrecked and it's a very different crowd than we see on Thursday nights," said Van Daalwyk.

The first Eve of Destruction drew a modest 1,200 fans. That number doubled the following year.

"We added more stuff to it the second year, like a jet car burn and some other novelty events," said Van Daalwyk.

By the event's sixth year, WIR was standing room only.

"The cars were lined up on the highway all the way to nearby Darboy. We had to turn people away that year," Van Daalwyk said.

The crowd was estimated that year at 15,000. People were sitting in the walkways and it became unsafe. Extra bleachers from the dragstrip are always brought in to accommodate the huge throngs of fans. The Eve of Destruction became such a big hit that WIR now sells advance tickets only for this event.

"We can hold 12,000 where we can get everyone in somewhat comfortably, and that way we can staff it better as far as food and drink, security and hiring from the sheriff's department," Van Daalwyk said.

The Eve of Destruction has become the biggest-attended event in track history. Van Daalwyk and Bunnell have shared their successful ideas with promoters at other tracks, and many other tracks across Wisconsin have some version of "The Eve" on their summer schedules.

Bus races are a popular draw at the Eve of Destruction events. (www.danlewisphoto.net)

*Jim Sauter (left) and ARTGO president John McKarns in 1981.
(Pete Vercauteren photo)*

WIR Honor Roll

Super Stock Track Champions

2020 – Shane Krueger
2019 – Wayne Sonkowsky/Greg Hauser
2018 – Rachel Meyerhofer
2017 – Dylan Wenzel
2016 – Dylan Wenzel
2015 – George Schwalbach/Terry Van Roy
2014 – Greg Hauser
2013 – Dylan Wenzel
2012 – Dylan Wenzel
2011 – Greg Hauser/Andy Casavant
2010 – Greg Hauser/Andy Casavant
2009 – Todd Bauman
2008 – Greg Hauser/Andy Casavant
2007 – Greg Hauser
2006 – Randy Van Roy
2005 – Andy Casavant
2004 – Andy Casavant
2003 – Andy Casavant
2002 – Terry Van Roy
2001 – Terry Van Roy
2000 – Chris LaRocque
1999 – Terry Van Roy
1998 – Randy Van Roy
1997 – Mike Rahn
1996 – Chris LaRocque
1995 – Chris LaRocque
1994 – Terry Van Roy
1993 – Terry Van Roy
1992 – Terry Van Roy
1991 – Terry Van Roy
1990 – Terry Van Roy

Sizzlin' 4 Track Champions

2020 – Scott Wolf
2019 – Beattie Brothers
2018 – Andy Miller
2017 – Dan Thomson
2016 – Mike Klein
2015 – Mike Klein
2014 – Wayne Sonkowsky
2013 – Ethan Beattie
2012 – Cory Romenesko
2011 – Cody Kippenhan
2010 – Wayne Sonkowsky
2009 – Tim Richter
2008 – Tom Schweitzer
2007 – Scott Verboomen
2006 – Nick Boldt
2005 – Phil Verboomen
2004 – Bryan Monday

Fox River Racing Club Super Late Model Champions

2020 – Bobby Kendall
2019 – Casey Johnson
2018 – Casey Johnson
2017 – Andy Monday
2016 – Jeff Van Oudenhoven
2015 – Lowell Bennett
2014 – Lowell Bennett
2013 – Jeff Van Oudenhoven
2012 – Lowell Bennett
2011 – Jeff Van Oudenhoven
2010 – Terry Baldry
2009 – Jeff Van Oudenhoven
2008 – Jeff Van Oudenhoven
2007 – Tim Rothe
2006 – Tim Rothe
2005 – Rod Wheeler
2004 – Terry Baldry
2003 – Terry Baldry
2002 – Terry Baldry
2001 – Terry Baldry
2000 – Terry Baldry
1999 – Terry Baldry
1998 – Lowell Bennett
1997 – Terry Baldry
1996 – Mark Schroeder
1995 – Matt Kenseth
1994 – Matt Kenseth
1993 – Terry Baldry
1992 – Jim Weber
1991 – Lowell Bennett
1990 – J. J. Smith
1989 – Scott Hansen
1988 – Scott Hansen
1987 – Scott Hansen
1986 – Scott Hansen
1985 – Scott Hansen
1984 – Terry Baldry
1983 – Terry Baldry
1982 – Terry Baldry
1981 – Jim Sauter
1980 – Alan Kulwicki
1979 – Alan Kulwicki
1978 – Rich Somers
1977 – Jerry Smith
1976 – Larry Schuler
1975 – Rich Somers

WIR Sportsman/Limited Late Model/Late Model Champions

1975 – Paul Lemke
1976 – Dennis Dietzen
1977 – Paul Jochman
1978 – Don Anderson
1979 – Al Golueke
1980 – Pete Berken
1981 – Pete Berken
1982 – Jim Duchow
1983 – Jim Duchow
1984 – Kurt Johnson
1985 – Jim Duchow
1986 – Rick Spoo
1987 – Dennis Dietzen
1988 – Rod Wheeler
1989 – Steve Smits
1990 – Rick Spoo
1991 – Rick Spoo
1992 – Mark Vanden Boogardt
1993 – Jeff Van Oudenhoven
1994 – Jeff Van Oudenhoven
1995 – Terry Korth
1996 – Terry Korth
1997 – Steve Smits
1998 – Steve Smits
1999 – Steve Smits
2000 – Dan Gracyalny   (last year on the quarter-mile)

2001 – Gary Natrop   (first year on the half-mile)
2002 – Doug Mahlik
2003 – Andy Monday
2004 – Tom Gee Jr.
2005 – Tom Spierowski
2006 – Kyle Calmes
2007 – Kris Kelly
2008 – Jim Duchow
2009 – Kris Kelly
2010 – Tanner Bohlen
2011 – Gary Natrop
2012 – Sawyer Effertz
2013 – Mike Meyerhofer
2014 – Corey Kemkes
2015 – Brent Strelka
2016 – Braison Bennett
2017 – Travis Rodewald
2018 – Jesse Bernhagen
2019 – Braison Bennett
2020 – Braison Bennett

WIR 1/4 Late Model Champions

2017 – Cory Kemkes
2018 – Cory Kemkes
2019 – Brandon Reichenberger
2020 – Tom Spierowski

Joe Verdegan

Acknowledgements

Writing a book and getting it edited and published can be a time-consuming project. There are numerous people who helped me put this book together that deserve a note of thanks.

At the top of the list is my wife, Kimberly. She was a most patient, supportive soul through the writing of my first book, *Life in the Past Lane*, and throughout the process of writing this book she's continued to be right by my side. I cannot thank her enough for the sacrifices she's put up with along the way. They were numerous and she's been supportive in more ways than I could ever have imagined.

When I first informed WIR's Roger Van Daalwyk that I intended to write a book about the race track he's grown up with, he was nothing short of being 100 percent supportive. Roger invited me into his home and had articles and artifacts he was willing to share with me – stuff that the general public hasn't seen. Roger, I hope I've done your race track justice through this book.

When it came to digging up a few facts, names and years, we received assists from Bob Abitz, Andy Monday, Dave Valentyne and Marty Nussbaum.

Former Fox River Racing Club president Mike Clancy hired me to be the track announcer at WIR, and for that I'm forever grateful. I am proud to say I had perhaps the best seat in the house on Thursday nights up in the announcing and scoring tower.

I would be remiss if I didn't give a shout out to the late Gary Vercauteren, who helped put WIR on the map with his tireless work, going to bat for the track with the local television and radio stations, and local newspapers. Gary fully understood how important it was to get the local race fans to the track. Gary was a true mentor of mine throughout my career of motorsports journalism. Gary's brother, Pete, a former *Midwest Racing News* columnist himself, was also a most valuable asset when it came to providing photos for the book. Thanks Pete!

Pete Vercauteren's assistance with providing photos to accompany the chapters has been nothing short of a huge asset. Pete shares the passion for racing in Northeast Wisconsin and I'm convinced he, too, could write a book of his own.

I would be remiss if I didn't give a shout-out to the voice of WIR, Matt Panure. I was fortunate to work with Matt and train him as a track announcer at Luxemburg Speedway. Matt wears many hats in the racing community and has assisted with getting in touch with people in this book.

Last, but most certainly not least, my publishers, Mike Dauplaise and Bonnie Groessl of M&B Global Solutions Inc. I learned a lot from my first book, but as my former advisor, the late Doc Snyder from the University of Wisconsin-Oshkosh would always say, "You never stop learning. If you think you know it all, you may as well pack it in." That saying holds true, and even while putting this book together, Mike and I were always trying to find ways to make this book one you'll never want to put down once you pick it up.

Joe Verdegan
Fall 2016

Joe Verdegan at WIR in 2016. (Ron Nikolai photo)

About the Author

Joe Verdegan has worn many hats in the motorsports industry in Northeast Wisconsin for nearly forty years, including a long-running stint as the motorsports columnist for the *Green Bay Press-Gazette*.

Verdegan has served as a track announcer at more than a dozen area race tracks, including Wisconsin International Raceway, a public relations man, race promoter, and marketing consultant for race promoters and drivers. He's been a color commentator for live television broadcasts on *Sports Showdown My32* as well as a racing columnist for *Full Throttle* magazine, *Midwest* and *Checkered Flag Racing News*. He was also the host of his racing program, *Track Talk*, on WCUB 980 AM.

Verdegan is a 1991 journalism graduate of the University of Wisconsin-Oshkosh. He has coached high school football at his alma mater, Green Bay Southwest High School, and resides in Dunbar, Wisconsin, with his wife, Kimberly. They have seven children and eleven grandchildren.

You can check out Verdegan's other books at his website, joeverdegan.com.

www.ingramcontent.com/pod-product-compliance
Lightning Source LLC
Chambersburg PA
CBHW071610080526
44588CB00010B/1086